STOP FAKING IT

START MAKING IT

Millennial's Guide to Real Wealth Creation

BY

JONATHAN TURNER

Ordering Information: Quantity sales. Special discounts are available on quantity purchases by corporations, associations, and others. Orders by U.S. trade bookstores and wholesalers.

DREAMSTARTERS

www.DreamStartersPublishing.com

Table of Contents

Dedication

This book is dedicated to my parents for disciplining me as a child, to my gorgeous wife Olivia, who deserves a Nobel prize for having willingly married me, and to you, the reader. Taking the time to read my book means the absolute world to me and I can only hope my passion for helping others is conveyed in the following pages.

Introduction

I'd like to start this conversation off with a public service announcement. If you're reading this book, I can promise you three things. First, I promise that while you certainly won't become a millionaire overnight, I can provide you with the right tools and the knowledge on how to use them to build wealth for your future. Second, I promise that while you may not become a globetrotting social media guru or a house-flipping stock trader with a fancy car, I can teach you how to create a secure and enjoyable lifestyle for yourself. Third, I promise that this book will be a reality check, a kick in the ass and a life altering conversation that needs to happen.

So, what does it mean to fake it in today's world? When you're faking it, you're trying to make something look more genuine and valuable than it really is. When you see a person continuously showing off their lavish lifestyle on social media, they could have gone into debt to obtain that lifestyle. That means they got money from the bank and used that money to buy some cool stuff that they can't afford. Now they're in a less than desirable financial situation all because they wanted a few extra likes for their profile picture. The scary part is that if you allow yourself to lose control with debt like that, it can absolutely crush you. Most people who are faking it don't realize that they could be using debt to their advantage, which is one of the things I'll get into later.

Have you ever been casually scrolling through social media and you're smacked in the face by an advertisement from a person claiming to be an expert in the financial field that can blow your mind and make you rich by next week? Of course, what they don't tell you is that to "get rich by next week", you'll have to pay a low upfront fee, and by paying that fee you still won't be getting rich by next week because it's just not that easy. If it were that easy, don't you think most of your peers would be rich already? Those ads are almost always put out there by people who are faking it. They want to make money by convincing you that their advice is the only advice you'll need to turn your financial life around in a way that's not possible in such a short amount of time.

Of course, there's always the possibility that you yourself may be faking it. That's right, you may be trying to obtain a lifestyle that you can't realistically afford. While you're out there showing off your expensive new car, your stomach is in knots because you can barely afford the monthly payment. Maybe you seem confident on the outside, but inside you really don't have a clear idea of what your future will hold financially. Yes, you could very well be doing yourself a great disservice by mismanaging your money and not giving a second thought to financial planning.

On the other hand, when you're making it, you're in the process of producing something. You're in the driver's seat of your life on a fresh strip of asphalt cruising towards your future. You've set realistic goals and have a clear plan of action to achieve them. You've got your windows down and you're enjoying the fresh air and scenery. Money no longer overwhelms you because you understand what to do with it. By taking control of your finances, you're taking control of your life and more importantly, your future. When you're making it, you have a realistic monthly budget in place that allows you to enjoy life responsibly. You have a healthy savings fund and a comfortable amount of money invested for your future.

Imagine for a minute, a future where you wake up feeling motivated about your career and have the sense of security that comes with a steady income and responsible spending habits. That's a nice thought, isn't it? Unfortunately for many of us millennials, we struggle with those feelings because growing up we weren't taught financial literacy in school. Even if you attended college, there's no required course on money management, and the closest you can get to that kind of knowledge is the advice of your most successful peers. And that's where I come in.

I'm Jonathan, a fellow millennial and a financial advisor with a love of cars, who is sick and tired of seeing so many fall victims to financial illiteracy. In my career, I pay close attention to topics that center around finance and investing. Overtime I noticed that as part of my job, I was focusing on people that were in the later stages of their career or at the beginning of retirement. Every day I was working to help people achieve their financial dreams by setting goals, managing their investments, protecting their income and assets, and planning their financial legacy. The only problem was, I was never working with people my own age.

Like most of my peers, I never paid much attention to everyone saying how financially screwed us millennials are. As young adults, we are not focused on the future in a way that allows us to prepare for it. So, while we may not be able to prepare for our future so easily, we should certainly see the reality of our current situation if we open our eyes to what's going on around us. The more I researched, the more articles I saw about millennials having no hope for a wealthy future and I realized just how big of a problem we're facing in this country. I also concluded that there's no formal financial education being taught to anyone to prepare them for the world we live in today. Even in my career field, there's a lack of education and service for our generation. It's clear that the financial industry these days is not catering to millennials and I feel that it's crucial to bring these issues to light.

So, what made me write this book? I want to help millennials understand the scale of our problems and that once we accept them, we can establish the necessary building blocks to change our future for the better. In this book, I'll give you jaw-dropping statistics, a few simple exercises to complete, and the knowledge and ability to understand the basic concepts of financial planning as well as the tools to build yourself a wealthier future. This book is meant to be a conversation on building wealth and taking control of your finances and the advice I give you can be used for the rest of your life. Trust me, your future self will thank you.

"At age 20, we worry about what others think of us. At age 40, we don't care what they think of us. At age 60, we discover they haven't been thinking of us at all."

Ann Landers

Chapter 1

Generation Screwed: Reality Check for Our Generation

It's time for a reality check for every millennial out there. As a millennial, you're part of the largest living generation of people in the United States, as well as a member of the fastest-growing generation in the American work force. But what exactly is a millennial and why does everyone seem to hate on us? The term millennial was first introduced in the 1991 book Generations, by Neil Howe and William Strauss. They coined this term to describe the generation of people that at their oldest, would be graduating high school in the year 2000, otherwise known as the start of the new millennium. Millennials are also referred to as Generation Y.

As millennials, we get a bad reputation in the media. We're accused of being entitled, lazy, overly sensitive, addicted to technology and social media, and completely dependent on Starbucks and avocado toast to make it through the day. Obviously not all of this is true, because I personally didn't even know that avocado on toast was a thing until recently. While most of us don't pay any mind to these judgements since we know they aren't true, there is one thing that's damn accurate. On any given day, you can find articles circulating the internet about just how financially screwed we as millennials are. Maybe they should rebrand us as Generation Screwed.

As a millennial myself, I began to research this on my own after seeing how many of us struggle financially. The result of my research was quite shocking. What I discovered is that there's a lack of financial literacy in our country of epic proportions. It's not only hurting us as millennials, but it's also hurting our elders and future generations. Right now, 78% of Americans are living paycheck to paycheck[1] and even more startling, over 50% of Americans don't have a savings fund in place[2]. It's estimated that the average American can only cover an emergency expense of around $400[3]. To make matters worse, over 70% of senior citizens have less than $60,000 in savings[4] with the average annual income for a retiree being under $50,000.

So just how screwed are we? While there are many topics that could be covered, I want to focus on addressing a few that I find to be the most shocking. It's a good thing you're sitting down to read this.

One statistic that doesn't generate enough attention from the media, is that the average net worth of millennials has plummeted 34% since 1996. In a nutshell, your net worth is everything you own (your assets) minus the debts that you owe (your liabilities). Assets include cash, investments, your home or other real estate, cars, and anything else of value. Liabilities are what you owe on those assets such as car loans, mortgages, and debt from credit cards or student loans. The average net worth for millennials today is less than $8,000[5]! Financially, that puts our generation behind previous generations when they were at the same age. Shockingly, our net worth is half as much as it was for our parents' generation at the same age.

So how the hell did we get here? As the cost of living continues to rise in the United States, our wages have remained stagnant. If we adjust for inflation, wages are only 10% higher right now than they were in the 1970's. That's an annual growth of just 0.2%, while inflation averages 3% each year. According to a study by Deloitte comparing data from 2007 through 2017, millennials are spending 16% more on housing, 21% more on healthcare costs, 26%

---

[1] According to a 2017 survey by CareerBuilder

[2] Based on Bankrate's January 2019 Financial Security Index Survey

[3] Report on the Economic Well-Being of U.S. Households in 2017

[4] CreditDonkey, April 2019

[5] According to Deloitte Future of Wealth Report

more on food costs, and 65% more on education. That last one really infuriates me because I can't comprehend what reason there would be for education to increase by 65% over a 10-year period.

At the forefront of this epidemic, we're earning lower wages than our parents did at the same point in their careers. The wages you earn in the early years of your career are often a large predictor for your future income potential, which makes this a very alarming issue. Currently it's estimated that our generation is earning 20% less than our parents' generation did at the same age. The economic crisis of 2008 through 2009, also known as the Great Recession, is a contributing factor of why we're in this position today. A recession is a period of stagnant or declining economic performance across an entire economy for two consecutive quarters. A survey conducted in 2018 showed the average household wealth for 23 through 38-year-olds was 25% lower than it was for a similar age group in 2007. Last year the Federal Reserve published a report that found the income of millennial households to be 11% lower than that of Generation X, or individuals born during the mid-1960s through 1981. Even worse, the Federal Reserve concluded that millennial households have an income that's 14% lower than that of the baby boomers, or individuals born during the mid-1940s through 1964[6].

As wages remain stagnant, inflation continues to make things more expensive for us, forcing many of us to finance our lives or take out debt just to survive. Inflation is the general increase in the price of goods and services over time. Remember when you were a kid and your mom paid less than a dollar for a pack of bubble gum in the checkout line? When you compare that cost to what you pay for a pack of bubble gum today, about $1.19, that's an example of inflation. The average inflation rate in the United States is about 3% each year, but many things have risen in price much faster. In 2017 alone, food prices rose 8.2%[7]. The cost of cable television rises on average by 6% every year, and from 2000-2016, the median US home price rose a staggering 96%[8].

---

[6] 2018 Millennials and Money Survey, Ameritrade

[7] United Nations Food Agriculture Organization, 2017

[8] United States Census Bureau

If we look at data, the average salary for a college graduate in 2018 was roughly $50,000 a year, or a little over $4,100 a month[9]. While that amount may not sound so bad, keep in mind that not all that $50,000 is yours to spend. This is your gross income, or the money you earn before the government takes out taxes. By the time your paycheck hits your bank, they will have taken out your local, state, and federal taxes as well as any employer deductions, like contributions to your employer's retirement plan or group life insurance, leaving you with a net income, or take-home pay, of just $40,000. It makes you wonder if they coined the term gross income because you're disgusted when you see how much of your hard-earned money gets taken out of your paycheck.

So now you're left with a net income of $40,000 per year, or roughly $3,333 being deposited into your bank account each month, but we still must account for where that money goes. So, blow the dust off your calculator and get ready for an eye-opening example of why so many of us struggle to make ends meet.

First enter the monthly net income of $3,333 subtract the following estimated amounts for monthly expenses.
- $1,400 for rent (current national average)
- $500 for your car payment, insurance, gas, etc.
- $250 for your phone, Netflix, internet, electric, etc.
- $400 for groceries, dining out, happy hour, etc.
- $200 for fun expenses, sporting events, movies, etc.
- $200 for personal care, health insurance, the gym, etc.
- $300 on material items like clothing, sneakers, etc.
- $389 on student loans (current national average)

Look at the number you're left with. Did you get -306? Yes, that's right, NEGATIVE $306. You didn't even come close to breaking even. Now imagine this happening every month. This is what most millennials experience as they struggle to make ends meet.

It's terrifying to look at these negative numbers and wonder how a person can survive each month, but they do. They survive because they finance their life by using a credit card or another form of debt to get by. But why would a credit card company willingly issue a line of credit to someone whose budget is so unbalanced?

---

[9] 2017 LendEDU Survey

Well, they're certainly not doing it out of the kindness of their heart, I can tell you that much.

You and millions of other Americans can get issued a credit card in this type of situation simply because they know you'll struggle to pay the minimum amount each month. That's right, in a sick way they are thriving by making a profit off your suffering. As your outstanding balance continues to grow, the credit card company continues to charge you a high interest rate as you continue to pay the bare minimum. Millennials carry an average credit card debt of $5,000 and an average student loan debt of $38,000. That means the average millennial is in around $43,000 worth of debt, and that's before factoring in mortgages, automobile loans, and personal loans[10].

Recent publications from the Federal Reserve have revealed a trend in rising credit card balances and delinquencies among our generation. That means more and more millennials are struggling to make even the minimum payments on their debt. In 2017, the Federal Reserve began to reverse a nearly decade long span of ultra-low interest rates, causing credit card interest rates to rise. This is a contributing factor in the rise of delinquencies among millennials, which hit an 8-year high in the beginning of 2019. So why did the Federal Reserve begin to put an end to such low interest rates? To understand this, you need to understand monetary policy.

Monetary policy is one of the ways the Federal Reserve attempts to control the economy. To simplify, monetary policy is an increase or decrease in the money supply (dollars) across our country. If the money supply grows too fast, the rate of inflation will increase and if the money supply grows too slow, the rate of economic growth can also slow. The actions of the Federal Reserve determine the size and rate of growth of the money supply, which in turn affects interest rates. Monetary policy is maintained by either increasing or decreasing the Federal Funds Rate or by changing the amount of money that banks are required to keep in their vault. By impacting the effective cost of money, the Federal Reserve can influence the amount of money that is spent by consumers and businesses.

---

[10] Morning Consult National Tracking Poll #190331

Think of the Federal Reserve as the foot on the gas pedal of our economy. If you press too hard on the gas pedal, you can cause the engine to rev too high and something critical can break. The same holds true for our economy. You can break the economy just like you can blow up an engine. On the other hand, if you let off the gas pedal too much, the engine revs may drop too low and the engine can stall. The Federal Reserve is trying to keep the engine running smoothly, by maintaining a balance in the economy always.

An increase or decrease in the money supply will in turn raise or lower interest rates for loans and credit cards. During a recession, the Federal Reserve would want to lower interest rates to rev up the engine, making loans for cars and homes more attainable and helping to influence the value of other investments like the stock market. During periods of expansion, the Federal Reserve does the opposite, and lets its foot off the gas pedal to slow down economic growth so the engine doesn't rev too high and break.

The United States had been going through a decade long expansion with the Federal Reserve, keeping their foot planted firmly on the gas pedal since 2009. In 2017 however, the Federal Reserve began to slowly take their foot off the gas pedal, using monetary policy to begin raising interest rates to slow down the economy. This caused an increase in interest rates, so your credit card interest rate went up and the credit card companies made more money off your outstanding balances. In 2008, the average interest rate for a credit card was 13%, while today, the average interest rate for a credit card is just over 18%. While these numbers are only an average, I personally know many people that are paying well over 20% interest on their credit card debt each month.

At this point it should come as no surprise to you that millennials are ill prepared for retirement. Over 65% of us don't even have a single cent saved for retirement[11]. If you happen to be in the minority of millennials that are saving for retirement, don't start to celebrate just yet because you may not be saving enough. The average retirement account for a millennial is just over $25,500[12]. With the life expectancy in our country on the rise, there is a very good possibility that our lifespans will exceed that of our parents'

---

[11] National Institute of Retirement Security, Millenials and Retirement 2018

[12] BankRate Financial Milestones Survey, 2018)

generation, meaning we will have many more years of expenses than they will. If you don't start planning and saving now, you'll need to work well into your golden years to survive, at a time when you may no longer be physically capable. But if you work hard now and plan appropriately for your future, you can enjoy your years of retirement without the stress of wondering if your next paycheck will be enough to get by.

Statistically, we're more educated than previous generations but it comes with a huge price tag. In high school our teachers and parents would tell us how important it was to go to college, so we could get great jobs and earn lots of money. What really happened is we took out student loans to earn a college degree and now we're busting our asses to pay that debt off for years to come, making us unable to enjoy our salary and a lifestyle we thought we could have. Talk about the strangest thing you ever did for money, right? Millennials have amassed more than $1.5 trillion in student loan debt. In fact, the average student loan debt per millennial is $38,000 with an average monthly payment of $389[13]. Personally, I know a lot of people that have an even higher balance with an even larger monthly payment.

Like I said before, this should be a huge reality check for you, but the good news is there's still plenty of time to improve your current situation and build a wealthier future. Time is on our side, as even the oldest millennials are only in their late thirties. If you start making changes today, you'll still have over twenty years of positive financial decisions to make as you work towards retirement. Retirement is another word for a work optional lifestyle. In a work optional lifestyle, you get to choose if you want to work as it's no longer out of necessity. If you'd like, you can choose to relax and enjoy your retirement because you've worked hard to put a secure financial future in place for yourself.

We as millennials are the most educated generation gracing this country, yet we're holding record amounts of debt, earning less than our parents, and are ill prepared for retirement. What else can be expected from a generation that was never taught proper money management? It's no wonder over 80% of us are living in debt with

---

[13] According to Debt.org

more than 60% of us living paycheck to paycheck[14]. We grew up without the basic knowledge about money management and proper financial planning, and if we don't start learning about it now, how are we expected to teach our children these same concepts in the future?

According to Forbes Business Development Council, we as a generation are set to inherit about $30 trillion dollars over the next 30 years[15]. This amount won't necessarily be equally distributed amongst us. Some will get a large amount of this inheritance and others may get nothing. This certainly isn't a golden ticket to a better future because if we don't properly manage the money we inherit, it could slip through our fingers in a matter of years. However, if we learn how to manage this money properly, we are looking at an accumulation of wealth this country has yet to witness and we can use it to build even more wealth on top of that.

I don't know about you, but that future is something I want to be a part of. I want to be proud of my generation and how we flipped the script despite poor financial literacy and a lack of guidance on money management. I want to be part of a generation that decided to use the advice of others to educate themselves on a concept that was completely new to them and then used that information to create a brighter and more successful future.

On a personal level, I want to be remembered as someone who changed the game in the financial world. I want to leave a legacy behind as someone that helped give a voice to a generation that had been passed over and written off by society. My goal with this book is to educate millennials about proper money management and financial planning so that we can all break the vicious cycle we've grown accustom to and begin thriving in our everyday lives. If we can successfully do that, then surely, we can change a hell of a lot more than just our finances.

I would argue that money management is one of the most important lessons we should be taught. Money runs the world and without it, you simply can't survive. Everything in the world has some sort of involvement with money from the house you live in to the water you use to brush your teeth every morning. One day, when

---

[14] Charles Schwab, 2019 Modern Wealth Survey

[15] Adam Bakhash for Forbes.com, August 2018

you're retired and living on a fixed income, how will you enjoy those luxuries that most of us consider basic needs if you can't manage your money and have no plan for retirement? Vacations, nice cars, and living a debt free life will always remain a dream for those of us that refuse to take action.

Personally, I feel that the basics of personal finance should be part of a standard curriculum in schools. How else are we expected to graduate, enter the workforce, and properly manage the money we earn? Instead, schools seem to prioritize the Pythagorean theorem and other things that we usually forget by the time we leave school for the day.

Sadly, there is no easy fix or overnight solution for this problem, but if we begin to prioritize our personal finances, we can use that knowledge as a tool to build a better future. I assure you that if you take the time to understand money and how to use it to build more wealth in the future, you can take back your life and own your finances instead of letting them own you.

I personally feel that this epidemic has been intentionally designed by a system that wants to milk us of every penny we earn. An educated population that makes smart financial decisions is a big problem for many of the financial institutions in our country. As they continue to make their riches from us, they'll influence and hinder any change that would negatively affect their bottom line. Now that we know what we're facing, we should really ask the question of how we got here in the first place. To answer that question, let's go back to school.

"Formal education will make you a living; self-education will make you a fortune."

Jim Rohn

Chapter 2

Class is in Session

Let's go all the way back to the beginning to where the problems first started; let's go back to school. The school system as we know it today is a lot older than you probably realize. The modern school system as we know it today, was created over 100 years ago, in 1902. Just let that sink in for a minute. The school system that's still in place today, was created in a time when there was no TV or internet, even the Titanic hadn't been built yet. Remember, this was a time before airplanes existed and neither of the world wars had taken place. It was at a time where we couldn't yet fathom putting a man on the moon and the most common form of transportation was a horse. That's over 100 years of the same education system.

The modern school system was created when John D. Rockefeller founded the General Education Board, which led to schools being modeled after factories, treating students like widgets and consequently teaching irrelevant information in place of focused lessons based on one's unique interest or needs. I'm not the first nor will I be the last to compare our school system to a factory. Some will argue against my views, but it's hard to deny the factory-like aspects of the American education system.

When you attended grade school, what was the first thing you did every morning after you arrived? You probably socialized a bit before a bell rang, signaling you to head to your first class, right? Eventually another bell rang, prompting you to head to your next class and when it was time for lunch, yet another bell would ring, and everyone congregated in the cafeteria to eat and socialize. You would repeat this process of bells, classes, and breaks until the final bell rang dismissing you to go home. Starting to sound a bit like a factory, isn't it?

The problem is that the assembly line approach of the American school system does not match with what we know about how people learn. Education psychologists have repeatedly argued that student curiosity and an adequate level of challenge are key factors in the learning process. Yet the typical school curriculum prevents us from pursuing genuine interests at an individual speed, and unfortunately, we're often forced to learn things at an inappropriate pace, inhibiting real learning and growth. I mean, when was the last time you used the Pythagorean theorem since you graduated?

My own personal experience in school was horrendous, and that's being generous to myself. I'm pretty sure that if any of my teachers from Middletown Area High School knew I became a self-sustaining, fully functional adult, they would faint. When they find out I've become an author, I'm almost certain some will go to an early grave from pure shock, seeing as how I didn't care to learn the required school subjects and was more interested in cars, engines, planes, and finances.

So why does this keep happening? Why isn't there a better system in place where students can thrive and learn more about how to function as an adult in the real world? In the late 1990s, there were only 25 states that required economic concepts to appear on their standardized tests. In the mid-2000s, the number of states had been reduced to 16 and today, there are only 5 states that require a personal finance course be completed prior to graduation[16]. I feel as if we're going the wrong way here, folks.

With the lack of financial literacy in schools, it's no wonder so many Americans are living paycheck to paycheck, with no money in savings, and only able to cover an emergency expense of $400[17]. It's also easy to see why most senior citizens have less than $60,000 in savings and the average annual income for a retiree is under $50,000[18]. The education system is certainly not doing us a favor by

---

[16] Champlain College 2017 National Report Card on State Efforts to Improve Financial Literacy in High Schools

[17] Economic Well-Being of U.S. Households Report, 2017

[18] The Balance, Retiring without savings at 60

keeping the basics of personal finance out of their curriculum; instead, they're setting us up for failure.

Luckily for us millennials, we're the most educated generation yet, with almost 40% of us holding a bachelor's degree[19]. If that's the case, why haven't we been taught all the important aspects of money management so that we can become thriving adults once we're out in the real world? One of the most important things a young person needs to understand when approaching the education system beyond high school is that things change in one very important and significant way, colleges are a business.

Colleges are in the business of making money and being profitable, and they certainly aren't handing out degrees because it makes them feel good. They hand out degrees because it adds to their bottom line. We were told as students that college was an investment in ourselves so that we could have a better future, but what if that isn't true for everyone? What if for many of us, that investment was a poor decision because after all, not every investment is a good investment.

Of course, for certain career fields like a doctor, lawyer, or nuclear engineer, college is necessary to receive a career-focused education. On the other hand, if you want to get into a skilled trade such as machining, electrical, or mechanical work, college might not be the best investment for you, as there are plenty of careers for those trades that pay well and don't require a formal college degree. For some careers, the requirements are more along the lines of basic work experience, a general knowledge of the field, and a few technical trainings and certifications, often provided by the company. If you end up with over $70,000 worth of debt with student loans for a career where you don't even earn $70,000 a year, college doesn't seem like such a wise investment. Wouldn't it have been nice to know that before you applied and took out a student loan? Shouldn't there be a way to explain that depending on your career and its income potential, a degree may not be as necessary for some as it is for others?

I want you to think back to when you were in high school. I'm willing to bet that your high school hosted a college fair when you were a senior. College representatives would come to your

---

[19] Pew Research Center, 2019

school and tell you what a great honor and prestige you would carry if you chose to attend their university. There were also quite a few bank representatives at this college fair, with each one of them smiling from ear to ear, eager to help you invest in your future with their very accommodating student loans. I'm also willing to bet that not a single representative from any college bothered to tell you that their school might not be right for your career goals, nor did any bank representative turn you away from their student loans.

The main issue that I see with our society today is that it plants the idea in our heads that we are required to go to college and get the value of a college degree to be successful and make something of ourselves. A college degree has become watered down to the point where it's basically the equivalent of a high school diploma. If everyone has a college degree, it no longer carries the same competitive advantage that it once did since we're all competing on a level playing field. But if you want to stand out today, colleges have an amazing solution for that. Once you earn your bachelor's degree you can pursue an even higher level of education with a master's degree or PhD. The solution is once again for you to put even more time and money into standing out amongst your peers.

Only 21% of our parents' generation has a college degree, but for millennials, almost 40% of us have earned a bachelor's degree.[20] Back when our parents were growing up, not only was college considerably less expensive than it is today, but it was also considerably more exclusive. Back then college was the solution to job security and financial well-being but that doesn't seem to be the case anymore in today's world.

I've repeatedly stated that we're the most educated generation and it's not by circumstance; we're the most educated generation by design. That's the main contributor for why we're in the hole for over $1.5 trillion in student loan debt. This all started decades ago in 1965 when the United States government passed the Higher Education Act. This Act was designed to encourage more Americans to attend college. It also marked when the government began to guarantee student loans provided by banks and non-profit lenders. It was less about educational improvements in our country

---

[20] Pew Research Center, 2019

and more about making money for the government, colleges, and banks.

To understand the purpose of the Higher Education Act, you must understand how a bank makes its profit. A bank makes its profit when you borrow their money and they charge you interest on it. When you pay off your loan, the bank stops making money off you. It's more beneficial to the bank if they continue lending you money to keep you in debt. I think the government grew a bit jealous when they saw how much money the banks were making, so they decided to enter the student loan business. To guarantee that they always get paid, the government made a rule that no matter what happens, you must pay back your student loans. You can't even declare bankruptcy to get out of your student loans. The only way out is to pay them off or pass away. Yikes!

Colleges and banks were ecstatic when it first passed because at that point they knew that they were always going to get paid regardless of the circumstance. They also knew that they could raise the cost of tuition to whatever they wanted. Colleges soon became like Oprah, handing out degrees to anyone in any field, saying "You get a degree, you get a degree, everyone gets a degree!"

There's just one flaw to this system and it's that the government has no damn money. In fact, the United States government spends hundreds of billions of dollars more than it makes and it's certainly not a profitable business because it doesn't sell any products or goods. So where does the money for these student loans come from? Look in the mirror because it's you along with every other taxpayer in the country. This is a win-win for not only the government, but also for colleges and banks.

Over 1 million people default on their student loans each year, which is a horrifying statistic, and by the year 2023, over 40% of all student loan borrowers are expected to be in default.[21] Being in default on a loan means that you've failed to make the required payment on its due date. In the media, there's a lot of debate as to what should be done about this and many are calling on the government to forgive the student loan debt. It sounds great in theory, but financially it will hurt every American more than it will help those with student loan debt. If the government wanted to pay

---

[21] Zach Friedman for Forbes.com, November 2018

off or forgive all these loans, they would need a lot of money, and remember that the government doesn't have any money. So, to get the money to pay off your loans, the government can try to borrow that money from other countries. Unfortunately, the United States already owes other countries trillions of dollars so that's not an option. The government could also sell government bonds, but by selling those bonds to raise money to pay for the loans, they still need to pay all that money back to the bond holders at some point.

There is one other solution where the government could just borrow the money to pay off your student loans from the Federal Reserve Bank. The only problem with that is the Federal Reserve is not a real bank and they don't have money either, but what they do have is magic. The Federal Reserve has magic that would make even Harry Potter jealous. While the U.S. Treasury Department actually controls and operates the printing presses, the Federal Reserve Bank effectively controls the money supply in the U.S. and can order new money be printed at any time. I wish I had that ability.

So, the government can borrow $1.5 trillion from the Federal Reserve and pay off all student loans, putting everything back to square one, right? Not exactly. This would result in two new financial issues. First, this would mean that the country's interest payments would go up because now we owe more money to the Federal Reserve. Again, the government doesn't have enough money, so to make up for these higher interest payments they'll need more tax money. And guess where that tax money comes from? That's right – the taxpayers! If the government did this, it would be the equivalent to you using a credit card to pay off another credit card, and only paying just the minimum payments on the new card. You'd be paying interest twice on the same amount of debt.

The second problem is that there's a secret cost to printing more money. When there are less dollars in the world, each dollar is more valuable. This is the same reason that some exotic cars are so valuable, because there are so few of them out there that it makes the demand for them higher. It's the same reason that a Honda Civic is less expensive than a Ferrari Enzo, because there are many more Honda Civics manufactured than there were Ferrari Enzo's.

By printing more money, the value of our currency goes down which makes the price of everything else go up, also known as inflation. So, if the government did pay off all student loans, sure there would be no more student loan debt, but now you'd have a higher tax bill. The cost of living would also skyrocket since we would have printed so much money. Like I said, the student loan crisis was not an accident and it's certainly not going away.

The only real solution is to pay down the loans as quickly as possible because if you have a loan balance, interest is being added to that balance which makes the government, colleges, and banks more and more money. That's a hard truth, but it's our reality and the bottom line is that most college students aren't just graduating with just a diploma, they're also graduating with a heavy burden of debt.

Now imagine for a minute that you had been warned about this before considering college. Imagine going to your college fair and above every college and bank, there was a warning sign that read "by attending our college, you may be doing yourself a disservice" or "by using our student loans, you will pay our bank for decades to come". Think about it this way; we're forced to see warning labels everyday about the foods we eat. Whenever I go to Chick-fil-A, I stare at a screen telling me how many calories I'm about to consume, yet there are no warning labels about attending college, the responsibility of student loans, or even credit cards.

What if you had a class your senior year of high school that discussed the pros and cons of attending college? What if in that class, a teacher would review career fields that both do and don't require a college degree and the average starting salary for the different fields? What if they also prepared students for the repayment of their student loans in the most efficient way possible? That would be great, but sadly, that class will never exist, because it wouldn't be good for the bottom line of the government, colleges, and banks.

Imagine the impact if you were taught in school how to balance a checkbook, invest in the stock market, understand inflation and compound interest, sell a product, negotiate, start a business, how to face failure, communicate with others, and even become a millionaire by investing just $5 a day! How about I give you a lesson that no school has ever taught anyone to date?

I can give you an example that will provide you with more value than 90% of the lessons you were taught in school. Let's look at how you could become a millionaire simply by investing $5 each day. For this example, you would take your $5 each day and invest it into the stock market, specifically the S&P 500, an American stock market index comprised of 500 large companies. Let's assume that your investment grows at an annualized rate of return of 8%. This is the average annualized rate of return for the S&P 500 throughout its existence. If you continue to do this every day for 50 years, you would grow your money to just over $1 million. Congratulations, you're a millionaire!

Take a look at the graph below to see how investing just $5 a day for 50 years would earn you just over $1 million.

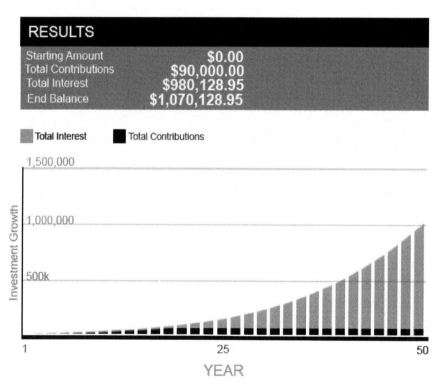

50 years is a long period of time, so let's cut that in half to just 25 years. Do you know how much money you would need to invest every single day so that in 25 years you'd be a millionaire? If

you doubled the investment amount and said $10 a day, you're wrong. You would need $40 a day to become a millionaire. By simply cutting the time in half, you can't just double the investment amount to arrive at the same destination and this is because of compound interest. If you're wondering how compound interest works, you need to first understand how simple interest works.

Take a look at the graph below to see how investing just $40 a day for 25 years would earn you just over $1 million.

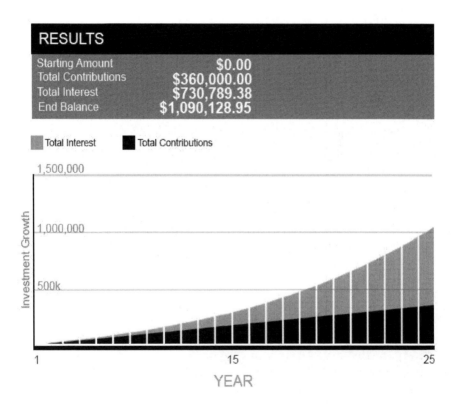

RESULTS	
Starting Amount	$0.00
Total Contributions	$360,000.00
Total Interest	$730,789.38
End Balance	$1,090,128.95

Simple interest is interest earned on the original principal only. Let's assume you invest $10,000 with 5% simple interest for 3 years. The interest you earn each year is 5% of your $10,000 investment. This equates to $500 a year, so over a three-year period, you would earn $1,500 in interest.

Compound interest on the other hand, is the interest you earn on your original investment (your principal of $5 per day in the first example or $25 per day in the second example) plus all the interest earned on the interest that has accumulated over time. Think of this as your interest earning interest.

If you were to invest $10,000 with 5% compound interest for 3 years, you would still earn $500 in the first year, but things would get more exciting in year two, when you earn 5% of $10,500. In year two, your interest would be $525 and if you add that to your investment you would end year 2 with $11,025. In year three you would earn 5% on $11,025 which equates to $552. In total, you earn $1,577; $500 in year 1, $525 in year 2, and $552 in year 3. It may not seem like a lot in this example but with compound interest you have earned an additional $77 versus using simple interest. The effects of compound interest become extremely powerful over a longer period, as the total amount of earned interest compounds, becoming larger and larger. This is why in the previous example you needed to invest $40 a day to reach your goal of $1 million in 25 years versus $5 a day for 50 years to reach your goal of $1 million. In the coming chapters, I'll show you exactly how to put this to practice in your life to begin building your retirement savings. This is just one of many valuable lessons that should have been taught to us in school.

Whether its grade school or college, there is not enough emphasis on financial literacy. Too often college is touted as a necessity for a better career with a higher income potential, and that's just not the case. I want to be clear that I'm not against college and while I believe that colleges are mainly concerned about making money, the career-focused education they provide can be extremely valuable for certain career fields. Equally valuable however are the experiences that you create while attending college. When I was a senior in high school, I would visit some friends who were already attending college at Penn State University Park. Talk about parties! After a few trips to see my friends, I made the decision before graduating high school that I wanted nothing to do with the constant party atmosphere, as it would only be detrimental towards the focus on my studies.

Imagine the shock on my parents' faces as I told them I wanted to stay at home while attending the local Penn State Harrisburg campus across town; it was priceless. I passed on the constant partying, choosing to focus on my degree and prepare myself to become a financial advisor. While attending the Harrisburg campus, I noticed quite a few cars that I thought were really cool. As someone who is very much into cars, I came up with an idea to create a detailing service for the cars on campus. This allowed me to meet other students and make a few dollars on the side.

These are the experiences I'm talking about creating for yourself in college. I chose to create an experience where I could not only meet and network with people but could earn money at the same time. Now what do you think I did with the money that I earned? Well, I certainly didn't invest a single penny, that's for sure. Instead I took the earnings and bought performance parts for my Nissan 350z in a futile attempt to make it the fastest car on the planet. Yep, I was an idiot. This was my first irresponsible decision when it came to cars, but it wouldn't be my last.

While attending college I was able to network with many of my professors and classmates over common interests in automobiles and racing. It was thanks to my college experiences that my mindset on making money helped shape my future. My college degree is nothing more than a piece of paper that holds no real value to me compared to my experiences, which gave me the idea to market myself in my career towards others that have the same passion for automobiles. Taking that practice into my career has helped me immensely to network and meet with new people.

When it comes to student loans and how to pay them off, there are a few things you need to understand. For starters, there is no one size fits all solution to this problem and it really depends on specifics like the amount of your student loan debt in relation to your income, whether the loans are public or private, and the interest rates of your loans. You should also keep in mind that the goals you set for your future can have a big impact on how you pay off your student loans. The good news is that today you will begin moving in the right direction with your student loans and that brings me to my next point.

Before you get too involved with paying down your student loans, you need to create a base cushion of cash. Remember when I mentioned the average American can barely afford a $400 emergency expense? Well, we need to be able to cover expenses like that first or else it's game over and you'll risk going into more debt just to save yourself. Initially, you should save up at least 1 month of living expenses, whether you keep it in cash or in the bank. Whatever you do, DON'T TOUCH THIS MONEY. This money should be enough to start you off with an emergency reserve and as time goes on the goal will be to get that emergency reserve up to 3-6 months of your living expenses. What would you do at this very moment if an emergency were to arise like your car breaks down or a pipe bursts in your basement? Would you have enough to cover at least some of the cost so that you aren't going into more debt to fix it? Thinking this way will help you form the habit of putting money away to avoid getting into more debt, which I'll expand upon later.

Once you've built your cash cushion you can move on to paying down your debt like your student loans and any credit card debt you have. If you owe money on a credit card with a high interest rate, you should focus on eliminating that debt first before you focus on paying off your student loans. Looking at your student loan debt next to your credit card debt may seem uneven since most of us owe far more on student loans, but the interest rate on your credit card is typically much higher than that of your student loans. Once you get yourself out of credit card debt, you'll have that monthly payment freed up to go towards paying down your student loan debt.

There are 2 main types of student loans; public and private. Public loans have a fixed interest rate, whereas private loans have a variable interest rate that can increase or decrease depending on the Federal Funds Rate. It's wise to first focus on any private student loans that you may have, as their interest rate is not going to stay in the same spot forever. Coming off a decade of low interest rates, it's entirely possible to see the rates of your private student loans increase in the coming years, which will cost you more money to pay off the same balance.

Once you have your private loans paid off, you want to prioritize your public/government student loan debt from the highest to lowest interest rate. By paying off the higher interest rate loans first, you save money in the long term with what you pay on the interest. Once you pay off the loan with the highest interest rate, you add that amount to the monthly payment of the loan with the next highest interest rate. This creates an avalanche of student loan debt payoff as time goes on.

All too often, our generation is so focused on paying down credit cards and student loans that we forget about our future. Maybe that's another reason why over 66% of us have nothing saved or invested for it[22]. I believe it's of the utmost importance to begin saving for your retirement as soon as you start working, even if it's just $5 a day. Life comes at you fast and before you know it, you'll be in the golden years of retirement, so if you start planning for those years today, you'll be far ahead of your peers when they reach that time in their lives. You always should be planning with your end goals in mind.

As you work on paying off your student loans, it's important to consider any other financial goals during this time and work on devising a place to achieve them. You should consider writing down those goals early on, so you can regularly remind yourself to work towards achieving them. Of course, life is unpredictable, and your priorities can change over time, but the important thing is that you'll be focusing on your future and making progress on saving and investing towards it.

You may not have a salary that gives you enough each month to keep up with your federal student loan payments and if that's the case, you may want to consider switching to a repayment program that's set as a percentage of your income. Remember that thanks to the government, you cannot discharge your student loans in bankruptcy, so a plan to pay them off must be established. There are a few options for these types of plans including Pay as you Earn, Income Based Repayment (IBR), and Income Contingent Repayment (ICR).

Introduced in late 2012, Pay as You Earn is the latest program designed to help students entering the job market for the first time in today's economy. To qualify for this program, you must have taken out your first federal student loan after September 30th, 2007 and had at least one disbursement after September 30th, 2011. A disbursement is when money is released from its source and in this case, it would be the government. This is typically the most affordable option of the repayment plans based off income. If you qualify for this plan, your payment is capped at 10% of your discretionary income, or the remaining money you have for

---

[22] National Institute on Retirement Security, 2019

spending, investing, or saving after paying taxes and necessities like food, shelter, and clothing. Any balance remaining after 20 years may be forgiven if you meet the requirements.

Income Based Repayment (IBR) is the next program to look at it if you don't qualify for Pay as Your Earn. In this loan program, your monthly payments are capped at 15% of your monthly discretionary income and any balance remaining at the end of 25 years may be forgiven if you meet all the requirements.

Income Contingent Repayment (ICR) is another program where your monthly payments are capped at 20% of your monthly discretionary income and any balance remaining at the end of 25 years may be forgiven if you meet all the requirements. There's something very important to know about IBR and ICR. If the government forgives the balance of your federal student loans, it's considered to be taxable income in the year the forgiveness happens. So, assume that you have $50,000 in federal student loans and are using IBR to repay your loans. After 25 years of making your payments on time, your balance is now $25,000. If the government forgives this amount, you will have to pay tax on that $25,000 as if it were income you earned in the year the loan was forgiven. That could potentially push you into a higher tax bracket and affect how much you owe on your taxes. Remember folks, there is no such thing as free lunch when it comes to the government.

If you are eligible to take advantage of any of these programs, your payment is recalculated annually as your income increases. The more money that you earn, the more money you must pay towards the loans. Also, if you qualify for one of these programs, you must never miss a single payment otherwise you're disqualified from them. So, if you take advantage of any of these programs, I would highly suggest setting up automatic payments to ensure that you never miss a payment. Another important thing to keep in mind is that the government can change any of these programs at any time, including how they're taxed.

There is another program, the Public Service Loan Forgiveness (PSLF) program, only available to those who work in the public sector such as for a public-school district, a hospital, or a government (local, state, federal) employee. In this program, after 10 years of making qualifying payments without being late and always making at least the minimum payment, the balance of your loan is forgiven. This is the only program where your income doesn't determine your eligibility. The 10-year span of making payments doesn't have to be consecutive either. This is also the only program that is not taxable when the balance of the loan is forgiven.

If you have qualifying student loan debt, you can deduct the interest that you paid on the loan during the year. For a student loan to be qualified it must have been obtained for the sole purpose of paying for higher education costs such as tuition, room and board, books, or meal plans. This deduction is capped at $2,500 in total interest per tax return, not per person, each year. If you're single, you can deduct up to $2,500 of student loan interest. If you're married and file a joint tax return, you and your spouse can only deduct a total of $2,500, even if you both have student loan debt. To take advantage of this you must earn under a certain amount of income. This amount may change on an annual basis. It is recommended to do your research on the income limits and consult with your tax professional to see if you could take advantage of this deduction. This amount of the deduction is also subject to change at any time.

I don't have a magic wand or the perfect answer for you if you have student loans, but I can tell you this; they aren't going away. There are currently over 45 million student loan borrows in the United States. Student loan debt can leave you feeling hopeless. If you're struggling to pay your student loans, don't just stop paying them! If you default on your student loans you could be sued, your credit destroyed for years, and even your income garnished by the government. A garnishment is when a court orders your employer to withhold a certain amount of your paycheck and send it directly to the person or institution to whom you owe money, until your debt is paid off.

My advice is not a one size fits all solution. You each have unique needs with varying levels of income, different types and amounts of debt, and different financial goals. These tips are just a basic framework to consider, and I recommend that you seek the help of a financial advisor to ensure you take the appropriate steps to become debt free while preparing for your future. The sooner you tackle this head on, the better, so devise a plan to pay your student loans down as quickly as possible. Luckily for you, we'll soon be chatting about the proper mindset to have and how to create effective systems to manage your budget.

You should now understand why so many Americans are living in debt and why so many millennials are living paycheck to paycheck. I've shed some light as to why the school system is the way it is and how we got into such a mess with student loans. Things are going to start looking up for you now and I say that because the knowledge and understanding of your current environment is a powerful tool. As you learn more, you'll be able to put those tools to use to create your future wealth. Now that you're on the right track towards a debt free future, the next question is would you rather look wealthy or be wealthy?

"Social media has become the millennial's financial Achilles Heel."

Allianz Life 2018 Survey

Chapter 3

Social Media – Friend and Foe

There's a reason I asked whether you would rather be wealthy or look wealthy and some of you may feel a bit defensive as you read this chapter. You might realize that you yourself have been trying to look and feel wealthy instead of taking the appropriate steps to eventually become wealthy. As a millennial, you're part of a diverse and influential generation. Social media has not only been created by this generation, but it's also been evolving at a rapid pace. The creation of social media has had both a positive and negative impact on our interactions with others and how we view the world. This chapter is all about how we portray ourselves on social media and how social media portrays the real world to us.

Millennials are known for allowing what we see on the screens of our smartphones to dictate what we do in our everyday lives. The average time spent by a millennial on social media is 141 minutes a day[23]. That's nearly 2 ½ hours on any given day spent laughing over memes, gasping at celebrity gossip, and gawking at other people's photos of their fancy cars (#carlovers), exotic vacations (#helloparadise), and highly-filtered selfies (#iwokeuplikethis). Social media is where we see photos of people that appear to be living their best and most lavish life.

I'm certainly not trying to bash social media because I do think it's one of the greatest technological advances of our time. I can think of no other invention that allows us to instantly connect in real time with someone across the globe or peek into other cultures right from our fingertips. Many of us are hungry for entertainment

---

[23] Charles Schwab Modern Wealth Survey, May 2019

and new information and there is no shortage of technology preventing us from doing that. If you use social media the right way, you can create many positive relationships and discover new and exciting opportunities for your life.

Let's take a more in depth look at the positive aspects of social media. Take this book, for example. There's a strong chance that it's because of social media that you even stumbled across it. Had you not seen someone share it on their page, scrolled by a photo of the cover, or had a friend message you the link to purchase it, you might not have known it even existed. Social media can connect us with new information and resources to better our lives. Face-to-face interaction are being replaced with posts, tweets, and hashtags. This can come as a blessing to family members that live across the country from each other. With the help of social media, extended family members can see photos of your children, get updates about your health issues, or congratulate you when they see the photos of your newly purchased home. Social media gives you the ability to communicate more quickly and more efficiently than ever before.

With billions of people around the planet constantly connected to social media, this has significantly impacted how businesses advertise and recreate the online shopping experience. We're able to get what we want when we want it, after seeing it pop up on our screen. In terms of marketing, social media is the most cost-effective way to reach a massive audience because consumers that support a product, service, or cause are more likely to share a post from their experience which further adds to the marketing potential for a brand.

As an individual, using social media to build a presence for yourself online by seeking out groups of like-minded individuals that share the same goals can be very beneficial. Thanks to social media, you can meet other people with your same passions that you would never have found otherwise. With a powerful network, you are no longer working alone but with an entire team that you can gain knowledge and insight from. Prior to writing this book, I had been involved in many entrepreneurship groups on Facebook. I have used those groups numerous times to get feedback on my ideas, listen to others' stories, and see what has worked and not worked for others in the past. Even the concept for this book stemmed from a social media group that has held me accountable to ensure I follow through on my promise to write it.

Social media is a very controversial topic at times and many argue that it doesn't provide any real value, but what I just described above shows that if you're using it the right way, social media can have a very positive effect at the individual level. Unfortunately, many millennials are not using social media to their advantage and instead, use it to competitively keep up with their peers, get the latest gossip, and see what their favorite celebrity is up to. While some of us post inspirational quotes (that we don't always follow ourselves) and hilarious memes for everyone's enjoyment, others are engaging in brutal disagreements over politics and airing their dirty laundry for the world to see.

One of the negative impacts of social media is how it affects our time management. Time is the most precious resource in our everyday life, because once you use it up, it's gone, and you can't buy it back or go back in time to do things differently. Many of us are wasting our precious time on things that don't help us financially or don't educate us on important aspects of life. I'll give you a great example that happened to me one day while I took a break from my daily routine. I began scrolling through my social media feed, which is normally comprised of personal finance articles, lots of cars, and the occasional sports update. While scrolling, I happened to come across a video of LeBron James shooting three pointers at practice. I flipped to the next video and there he was again, practicing his free throws. I eventually came across a video montage of his greatest moves and before I knew it I had spent 45 minutes of my valuable time watching videos of slam dunks. It had no valuable impact on my life except that it robbed me of 45 minutes of my day that I can never get back. Those 45 minutes could have been spent more productively by generating revenue for myself and my business, but instead I was sucked down a rabbit hole. An occasional break from the monotony of daily life is fine, but when you have a long list of things to accomplish for the day and limited time to tackle them, 45 minutes for an entertainment break is time wasted.

When was the last time you found yourself aimlessly scrolling through your phone, checking your Facebook feed, liking Instagram photos, or watching YouTube videos? I bet it was within the last hour or two since that's the norm for us as millennials. Like zombies, we open our apps and start scrolling aimlessly to distract ourselves from the stresses of our life but doing this too often can hinder your productivity and your ability to grow. When you allow social media to monopolize your time, you're doing yourself a great disservice.

In the next chapter, I'll get into more detail about another major issue with social media, and that's the rise of social media scams that many of us fall victim to. All too often, we come across an "opportunity" on social media to make our lives better and get us rich. Whether you're a stay at home mom that is limited to the types of jobs she can take on, or someone who is just tired of being in the traditional work environment of reporting to someone and meeting a quota each month, these types of opportunities can be very appealing at first glance. They'll tell you that you can be your own boss and work your own hours and this appeals to millennials right away because of course we want more time to do the things we love instead of working. They make it seem as if you can make a ton of money by only working a few hours a week. These opportunities and the people that put them out there are not being genuine because in the end, you will still have a boss (yourself) and if you're not disciplined enough, you won't end up working enough or properly marketing your goods or services to even make a profit. No matter what anyone tells you, there will always be some sort of quota in any line of work, whether it's how many goods you make, how many products you sell, or how many new clients you sign. You can't make money if you aren't making your quota just like if you don't sell enough vehicles as a car salesman, you may not be making enough off commission to keep up with your monthly bills. The truth is that there is no easy way to get rich quick so when it comes to opportunities on social media to make money this way, remember that if it seems too good to be true, it probably is.

Of course, when it comes to the negative impacts of social media on millennials, perhaps one of the biggest issues is how it influences our spending habits. According to a recent study, nearly half of millennials surveyed have admitted that their spending habits are directly influenced by the photos and experiences that we have through social media[24]. How else can we see how great a shiny

---

[24] HLoom, United States of Financial Waste Survey

leather recliner looks in our home without seeing it first in someone else's living room? We get these types of experiences from our peers, our favorite celebrities, and even from complete strangers. Over half of the group surveyed admitted that they had bought something that they'd seen advertised on social media without having any intention to purchase it prior to that. All it takes is for a celebrity or someone we admire to recommend a product and we're immediately pulling out our credit card. Why else do you think your favorite brands have celebrity spokespeople or well-known social media influencers promoting their products? They know that when we see this, we expect to have the exact same experience they did.

In that same survey, 90% of millennial participants said that social media creates a tendency for them to compare their own wealth or lifestyle to that of their peers. If you spend all your time trying to keep up with the Joneses, you are assuming you can afford the lifestyle that someone else can afford. Even worse, many of the people showing off their luxury lifestyles are in a bad financial situation (#noleasedlambos), but you would never know that because you aren't behind the scenes.

Remember, if you need to work 20 hours a day to afford the payments on something just so you can have what someone else has or flex on social media, you're not wealthy. Having nice things and being wealthy are two completely different things. Just because you have an expensive hobby or go on expensive trips, doesn't mean you're living within your means and you may not be making practical spending decisions. Some people that we view as having lots of money or wealth are not actually portraying their genuine self. These people could have massive debt and no money invested for their future. Never compare yourself to someone else on social media. Even I have been guilty of comparing myself to someone who portrays themselves as more successful than myself and I am not alone because when surveyed, 88% of millennials said that they compare themselves to others on social media as well[25].

Everyone is in a different position in their life and what is realistic to one person may not be realistic to another, but social media allows us to mask the reality of our situation, so it's a poor way to judge a person's reality. Social media also feeds into our

---

[25] Allianz Life, 2018 Survey

need for instant gratification because when someone has something we really want, we can instantly click a link and make a purchase regardless of if we can afford it or not. This satisfies our urge for instant gratification.

Social media has absolutely distorted the way we view success. These days, success is viewed as an enormous mansion, an exotic car, or a tropical vacation home. The truth is that success shouldn't be associated with a set standard of possessions or money. Some people view being successful as being able to afford their 1,000-square foot home, feed their 2 children, provide them a great education, and enjoy a reasonable vacation once every few years. For others, success may be a nice car and a second home they can use for vacations several times throughout the year. Other people's success is too often glamorized on social media and it makes us forget our original goals and what we deem necessary for ourselves to be successful. Sure, to some people a vacation home may seem cool, but if you're not someone that likes travelling, why do you feel like you need to be on that same level? Social media makes it harder for us to reflect on our own situation and the simple things in life that make us happy.

Like I said, there's nothing wrong with a huge house or a fancy car, but we shouldn't view those things as indicators of success in and of themselves. If you get too caught up chasing after them by going into massive amounts of debt to get them, you're drastically jeopardizing your future. In a later chapter, I'll explain both the right and wrong way debt is used to obtain these types of things.

There are warehouses that exist where smartphones, as far as the eye can see, are plugged into a server that is generating fake profiles, fake likes, fake product reviews, and fake experiences for people on social media. While there are plenty of social media influencers with a large following that have worked hard to earn their fame the right way, there are far too many that have completely cheated and faked everything to grow a large audience. There are even companies out there that exist for the sole purpose of turning your social media account into a sales funnel full of fake followers, less than genuine reviews, and completely irrelevant customer interactions, all for a set fee. This is what enables some of the so-

41

called "influencers" we know to create such a large following and shows the lengths people will go to just to become #instafamous.

One way to consider using social media to your benefit in today's digital world is using it to make money. There are many ways to use social media to make money, all from the comfort of your smartphone. It's estimated that 2 billion people currently use social media, so you have the potential to reach a lot of people if you present yourself or your products the right way. If you're going to be scrolling through social media every day, you might as well make some money while doing it.

It's important to understand that every business needs paying customers to survive, and these customers are regular people that likely spend a lot of time on social media. That means that if you can build a large social media following with people that share your same interests like travel, fitness, cars, fashion, or home décor, you already have an audience interested in your niche. This makes them potential customers for the products or services you offer, and the stronger your following, the more money you can make simply from advertising. If this type of business venture excites you, consider doing more research on how to organically grow your social media following and monetizing it.

As an example, let's say you use social media to post automotive repair tips and tutorials and you have a following of around 10,000 people. It's obvious your audience is interested in cars, so now you have a few potential ways you can make money. The first way is advertisements and sponsorships. Businesses and brands are always looking to get more exposure and the future of advertising is no longer TV and radio, but through social media. When you build up a group of loyal followers in your niche, you become a social media influencer and it's possible for you to partner with an automotive repair brand for example and promote their products to your followers. This is usually done for a set fee that's paid by the brand you're working with. Of course, there are a lot of advertising and endorsement laws and guidelines out there so make sure you do your research and consider speaking with an attorney in your area.

Another way to make money on social media is by becoming an affiliate for a brand. As an affiliate you earn a commission based on the sales that company gets through your individual coupon code, affiliate portal, or referral link. This type of venue requires more work because you need to understand how to market the products your promoting or selling. Unlike a paid sponsorship, there is no limit to how much you can earn from your sales over time so if you have a big following, you can likely get a lot of sales with little advertising costs.

When you build a brand using social media, the possibilities can be endless. Keep in mind however that the things you sell or services you offer must provide a value to the people purchasing them or else they won't have a need to make a purchase. Building a brand isn't just about selling things, it's about meeting the needs of your customers.

Social media can be your best friend or your worst enemy depending on how you use it. If you use it as a tool to better yourself and give yourself a bigger voice, it can substantially help you. If you use it to compare yourself to others or to try and keep up with Joneses, you're not going to gain anything except debt.

You don't always have to use social media as a tool to make money either. For some careers like a biochemist, your job doesn't require you to impress your followers with your skills through social media. You may simply enjoy using social media to keep up with your friends' lives as they get engaged or buy a house or just to scroll through hilarious memes on your lunch break.

As I said earlier, properly using social media has been very beneficial to me as I've been able to connect with other like-minded individuals around various business topics and ideas. Social media has been crucial for the creation and promotion of this book! As with everything, social media has its fair share of drawbacks. An important aspect of social media that needs to be discussed is how it presents us with opportunities, that at times are just too good to be true.

"Get-rich quick schemes are for the lazy and unambitious. Respect your dreams enough to pay full price for them."

Steve Maraboli

Chapter 4

There's a Sucker Born Every Minute

"How would you like to pay off all your debt, own your dream car, pay off your mortgage early, or own a vacation home?" "Great, I can show you how! For a one-time fee, I'll give you all the secrets and unlock all the doors that will earn you massive wealth!" Sounds familiar, doesn't it? We've all seen ads like this on social media. You're scrolling through your newsfeed or searching for something on the internet, when one of these "amazing offers" smacks you in the face. I'm constantly bombarded by these types of offers and I'm going to call them out for what they are, scams. They are preying on your money and your desire to attain wealth by giving you a false sense of ambition that it can be done overnight.

Well-marketed scams aren't the only way we're being sucked into a bad investment. Even before today's technology, someone could dupe the masses simply by creating a state of mania around a certain business, product, or investment where everyone would rush into the new venture in the hopes of becoming wealthy without first doing their research and ending up in a worse financial position then when they started. This has been happening for hundreds of years and the worst part is that a mania can happen over the most ridiculous things. A mania is when something is peddled, pushed, and hyped up so much that it catches the attention of the masses. The mania goes up and up until it explodes, causing a lot of people to lose a lot of money. Take for instance, tulip mania, when people were going crazy over something as simple as a flower.

Tulip mania occurred in the 17th century and is the first recorded asset bubble. An asset bubble is when the price of an asset, such as real estate or stocks becomes over-inflated. Prices rise quickly over a short time period and the increase in price isn't supported by an underlying demand for the asset itself. When investors bid up the price beyond any real sustainable value, they create an asset bubble. A great indicator of an asset bubble is irrational optimism, where almost everyone is buying an asset based on an implied demand and a notion that it will continue to increase.

In the 1630's, French merchants began to buy tulips for their wives, making them appear to be a luxury item. This caused the sellers of tulips to begin stockpiling them, which increased the price for growing and harvesting due to the implied demand. People believed they could buy tulips in large quantities and sell them for a profit, and it would be a sound investment. Of course, this wasn't the case, but people didn't do their research and instead everyone rushed out to buy tulips. Through the winter months of 1636 into 1637, the price of tulips shot through the roof from the implied demand. A tulip could fetch around 2,500 guilders, a form of currency, which was the equivalent to 16 and a half years of pay for skilled work! Wise investors began to see the market was unmanageable and stopped investing their money into the tulips. In February of 1637, the bubble burst when a tulip auction in Harlem failed to attract a single buyer. The merchants who still held the tulips went into a panic and tried to quickly sell off these worthless flowers causing the price to drop significantly. It was made even worse because many florists had been selling tulips they did not yet own to buyers who couldn't afford them. Many people were left in financial ruin over this mania and it all happened in the blink of an eye.

As a kid, you may remember the collection of Beanie Babies most of us had, which is a great example of a mania we all lived through as we watched it happen to our parents. Parents rushed out to get Beanie Babies after reading that they could become very valuable someday. They were banking on the idea that years down the road, people would be looking to pay top dollar for these toys. Stores were stock piling Beanie Babies and parents would get into fights with one another over the ones they believed would be the rarest ones someday. Inevitably, Beanie Babies did not hold their value and the bubble burst which left many families with a stock

46

pile of beanbag toys and children that eventually grew out of their interest in playing with them.

That's why you should never get caught up in mania or invest in something with the notion or idea that you want to make a quick buck, because it's just not sustainable. Like I said, there are countless scams out there so let's look at another example of how we as the masses can get sucked into something that's just too good to be true.

Thanks to social media, there's a misconception about how to make money in a short amount of time that's really skewing our perception of reality. We're often shown things happening very quickly on social media, when in reality things don't happen that fast, and accumulating wealth is one of them. Simply put, you cannot create wealth overnight because it's just not possible. But when social media shows someone else that claims to be doing it, we suddenly think it's possible and we see this everyday both on and off the internet.

Millennials are being fed a false sense of hope that they too can become massively successful overnight. Who can blame us when we're being bombarded by ads showing someone on a white sandy beach, flying in a private jet, or suddenly living a debt-free life? Of course, they don't bother telling us that those jets are leased, the beach house is rented, and their debt-free life is in fact massively leveraged. While we would all love to have some of those things in our own lives, we're being fed a false sense of security and accomplishment for achieving them.

Let's look at some of the most popular scams and manias that are present in today's world. The first would be Multi-Level Marketing (MLM) schemes which are when people either buy the right to sell a product or they purchase the actual inventory of a product after being recruited by someone else. If you have any type of social media account, there's a good chance you've seen an MLM scheme come across your feed, whether it's clothing, makeup, health supplements, or cleaning products. While MLM schemes have existed for decades, they have become easier than ever to get sucked into thanks to social media. Rather than focus on selling the products, many people focus on recruiting more people to sign up under them as a seller, which builds a pyramid like structure where the people at the top are making money off everyone that signs up at every level below them. It's very easy for so many people to get sucked into signing up, because they're falsely convinced that it's an opportunity to make money and be their own boss. The problem is that selling any product requires some training or background with marketing. Many of these companies don't invest in providing training to everyone who signs up, because the truth is, they don't care if you're a bad salesman because they still make their money when you sign up. And if you convince others to sign up, they'll make money from that, too. 99% of all MLM recruits end up losing money[26] because most of the commissions end up going to a very few of the top promoters at the top of the pyramid structure. On top of that, 50% of representatives end up dropping out after a year. Currently, there are over 18 million Americans involved in one of these schemes[27].

Another well marketed scam is individual stock picking. There's an entire industry out there built on this idea that there are those who can give you special insights into the performance of any given stock that will help you outperform the market. But statistically that is not true and more importantly, most of the time those that participate lose money.

Before we can talk about these types of scams we must first understand the basics about stocks. Stocks are a type of investment that represent an ownership share in a company. For companies, issuing stock is a way to raise money to grow and invest in their business. For investors, stocks are a way to grow their money and outpace inflation over time. When you own stock in a company, you are called a shareholder because you own a portion of the company's stock. Public companies, ones that issue stock, sell their stock through a stock exchange like the New York Stock Exchange. The stock exchanges track the supply and demand of each company's stock, which directly affects the stock's price.

It's important to remember that if you're going to buy a stock based on a prediction that it will do well in the future, it should never be about a short-term benefit. Chances are if you have access to information on a stock, so does the rest of the market, and it's most likely already affected that stock's price. You should always

---

[26] The Case (for and) against Multi-level Marketing, by Jon M. Taylor, MBA, Ph.D., 1999

[27] What Are the Top MLM Companies in 2018?, by Megan Elliot, 2019

think in the long term. For example, you might be thinking that a certain industry, like data storage, is going to be more widely used over the next decade. That could be a good opportunity to use some of your personal insights and research to form a decision. Investing is all about steady, slow, long-term choices. If you ever happen to stumble upon secret information about a stock that allows you to make a valuable investment choice, that's called insider training and it's illegal. Insider trading is why Martha Stewart went to jail, and you don't pass go OR collect $200 when that happens.

The reality is that most people that participate in stock trading programs are losing more often than they're winning. With these scams, you're being pushed an "investment" program that will try to convince you that you'll be trading just like Bobby Axelrod from the show Billions in no time. This is predominantly pushed through penny stock trading, day trading, and Forex trading courses and watch lists. Let's look at each one in more detail.

Penny stocks are stocks that trade below five dollars. These types of stocks are often associated with small companies and because they trade infrequently they lack liquidity. Liquidity is the ability to easily convert an investment to cash in a short amount of time. As a result, investors of penny stocks may find it difficult to sell stock since there may not be any buyers at that time. Due to their lack of liquidity, penny stocks are generally considered highly speculative. In other words, investors could lose a sizable amount or all their investment.

Often, you'll see individuals claiming to have insight on the penny stock market. These penny stock "experts" have created a very clever scheme that many fall victims to. They market themselves to individuals by creating a notification system through email or text that, for a small fee, promises you the best time to purchase or sell penny stocks for massive profits. What many of these "experts" really do is seek out a penny stock that has little to no active buyers, then begin to purchase shares of the stock over a period of a few months to make the stock appear to the public as if it's active. These so-called experts want the stock they're about to push to attract attention from other investors, giving their recommendations credibility. At this point, the "experts" release a notification to their subscribers to purchase the stock in question.

Many of the subscribers purchase the recommended stock, creating a bubble due to so many investors purchasing it at the same time. This causes the share price of the stock to rise higher and higher. At this point the "experts" begin to sell their shares of stock that they originally purchased, for a massive profit. The "experts" then send out a notification, days or weeks later suggesting to their subscribers that they should sell the stock as well.

Once the alert goes out to sell the stock, everyone wants out at the same time. Remember, liquidity is only available if someone else is willing to buy what you're selling. If the stock that you're selling has no new buyers, the price drops very fast causing the bubble to burst. In these scams, people following the alerts have the potential to make money depending upon how quickly they act but what many don't realize is they're making the "experts" a hell of a lot of money in the process. There are countless instances where someone has followed the recommendations of an "expert" alert system only to see their investment evaporate.

Other examples of these types of scams can be seen in day trading or Forex courses where internet marketers and gurus tell you how much money you can make and how easy it is to do so. They claim that if you listen to them, you only need a few bucks to start and you'll be making millions in no time. Day trading is often made out to be more glamorous than it really is and is primarily pushed with a promise that an "expert" will teach you how to trade in exchange for a small fee.

A day trader is a trader who buys and sells the same stock multiple times a day to capture that stocks increase and decrease in price movement. This is called price action and it's a result of temporary supply and demand inefficiencies caused by purchases and sales of the stock by others. There are no special qualifications required to become a day trader and day traders usually buy or sell their shares of a stock on margin. Margin is a type of account where you use borrowed money in the hopes of reaping higher profits through leverage. You also run the risk of higher losses too which is why many people who start down the road to becoming a day trader, eventually become part of a statistic. 90% of traders fail to make money when trading in the stock market[28]. This statistic deems that

---

[28] Trading the Stock Market, Wealth Within, 2018

over time 80% lose money, 10% break even, and 10% make money consistently.

Forex is a marketplace where various national currencies are traded such as the US Dollar, the British Pound, and the Chinese Yuan. The Forex market is the largest and most liquid market in the world, with trillions of dollars changing hands each day. This market is an electronic network of banks, brokers, financial institutions, and individual traders where everyone is attempting to speculate on the direction of a pair of currencies, such as the US Dollar vs. the British Pound. A rarely advertised fact is that most Forex traders fail. In fact, it is estimated that 96% of all Forex traders lose money and end up quitting[29]. To make it simple, Forex trading is simply betting on how one currency will change in value compared to another. When you are trading Forex, you want the currency that you're holding to rise in value compared to another country's currency so that you can make a profit.

For most people, day trading and Forex trading are a terrible idea. It takes a lot of time, effort, and expertise to make it in these markets. Being successful is no joke and it's not easy when you're jumping into any of these markets with no real experience. You are immediately competing against professionals, banks, and with Forex, even against entire countries as they hedge their currencies. Jumping into day trading or Forex trading is the equivalent to playing pro basketball against LeBron James having never played a single game of basketball in your life. Most new day traders and Forex traders don't understand the markets or how trading works. Just because markets and trading are easily accessible from your smartphone, doesn't mean it's easy to make money.

When you trade, you're competing against the best in the world and only the best make money while the rest are simply providing that money to them by losing on a trade. For the select few that want to make trading their entire career, you need to do it day in and day out. Day trading and Forex trading have the potential to make you money, but that doesn't mean it's going to happen, and it's that potential that you see all these internet marketers and gurus so often selling.

[29] Reasons Why Forex Traders Lose Money, The Balance, 2019

The market is not something you can beat but rather something you must understand. Having a "beat the market" mindset often causes traders to trade too aggressively, ignore warning signals, and ending in financial disaster. Something to keep in mind about anyone attempting to market themselves as a trading expert in any of these markets is that if they are selling to you on social media, they're faking it. Why would they waste their time to sell you a course for a few hundred dollars when instead they could sell their information and techniques to large financial firms for hundreds of thousands of dollars?

A recent example of a mania was that of cryptocurrency and blockchain in the Fall of 2017. Now, cryptocurrency in and of itself is not a scam nor is blockchain technology. Cryptocurrency is the actual currency and blockchain is the technology that allows for currencies to operate. In the months and years prior to the Fall of 2017, many people began to believe cryptocurrency was an important tool for us in the digital age and began to invest in it. As its prices rose, more and more people started to notice and by the Fall of 2017, cryptocurrency mania was in full swing, even being broadcast on major news outlets. Many were hyping up cryptocurrency as a relatively solid investment and a way to get rich quickly. There were cases of people re-mortgaging their homes, pulling out all their money out of their bank account, or liquidating most of their other investments accounts to buy into cryptocurrency in the belief that it would continue to rise. The bubble burst in a spectacular fashion in the early months of 2018 and has not yet recovered to its previous high. We will see what the future holds for cryptocurrency and blockchain.

I want you to visualize building your wealth like becoming a bodybuilder. You will never see a 130-pound person without any muscle tone, wake up one day in the hopes of becoming a bodybuilder and accomplish it in just a week's time. It takes years of dedication with a strict meal plan and commitment to a strong workout regimen to get the physique to become a bodybuilder and step on stage, and your personal finances are no different. You cannot cheat your way to the top because it's just not feasible and it takes years of dedication, hard work, and consistency to achieve your best financial physique possible.

One thing you will never see on social media, is someone reliable and trustworthy making you promises for instant wealth. We see countless people on social media talk about how if you do what they tell you to, you can have a million followers, successfully invest in the stock market, or become an expert at flipping real estate. Many of these people sending this message have a fake social media following, post anything but legitimate reviews, and are not being honest with themselves or their audience.

Instead of investing in your own future, when you fall for their scam, you're making them wealthy and you're left scratching your head with nothing left to show for it. In a later chapter, we will focus on the stock market and ways that you can properly use it, but before we get to that, we need to discuss what money is and its purpose in the first place.

"It's good to have money and the things that money can buy, but it's good, too, to check up once in a while and make sure that you haven't lost the things that money can't buy."

George Lorimer

Chapter 5

What is Money?
What is Wealth?
What's the Point?

Money in its earliest and most basic form, was a bartering system. Back then people would literally trade one object for another based on their perceived value of each object. As society grew larger, this type of system couldn't be supported and that's when money as we know it today was created. Money has taken the form of animals being traded back and forth, as rocks and shells being exchanged for goods, and eventually as metals like silver and gold. Metal coins held the form of money for a very long time until it transitioned into the paper currency we use today. Even our paper money has evolved as most of our money today is nothing more than a few digits on our computer or phone screen.

With money today, if you were to open your wallet, the paper currency inside holds no more value than any other piece of paper. Have you ever heard the saying that the money in your wallet is worth less than the paper it's printed on? That's because a $100 bill itself is worthless but the perception of it gives the $100 bill its value and it's the government that tells you that a $100 bill is worth $100. The value of our money exists only when we, as a society, agree to the assigned value of the paper.

So, in a sense, money is almost an illusion. The reason our money has value is because people believe that it does. You believe that your $100 bill has value and you are willing to give it to the store clerk in exchange for a new pair of shoes. Our money is not backed by anything; there is no object or material of true value such as gold that is backing it. Yet, people spend their entire lives chasing this illusion of money partly because it's what society wants us all to do. You're told you must go to college to get a well-paying career to earn money. Money is dangled in front of you like a carrot, so you put your blinders on and you chase that carrot in the form of a paycheck. You're always trying to get that paycheck higher and higher. When you get a bonus, for example, what is the first thing you do with it? Most people go out to buy themselves something new like a TV, laptop, or some new furniture. But couldn't you be doing something better with it, something that would be more valuable?

Fundamentally, spending money isn't bad and it only becomes an issue when it's spent mindlessly purchasing things that you don't necessarily need and that only bring you temporary happiness. Money can't make all your problems disappear because money is often what serves only to highlight our internal struggles. This happens because we're spending our money ineffectively and inefficiently while trying to chase after the things that don't make us happy in the long run. That's a very big psychological aspect to money that isn't taught to us.

The first thing you need to do for yourself when it comes to how you think of money is make sure you align your definition of money and your spending of money with your values. How you spend your money should be in unison with what you believe is most important in your life. That's obviously easier said than done but by first identifying your values, you can take a deeper look at your life.

You need to be honest with yourself about what your values are and the goals you have for your future. You must also accept what it takes to achieve those goals and then create and set priorities in a structure that allows you to attain them. Once you do that, you'll start to notice how spending money can be unnecessary at times. Maybe you were going out to eat on a weekly basis and you suddenly realize it's taking money away from achieving one of your goals. This is why you need to know what truly makes you happy. Is it the meal you eat or is it the atmosphere of the restaurant and the company you're with? Maybe you can find other ways to feel that happiness by having family or friends over to your place and asking everyone to contribute by bringing a dish. This saves you as the host some money but still allows you to enjoy good company and a fun atmosphere.

Making changes like this can show you how unnecessary it is to spend money in certain ways. You need to understand what truly makes you happy and fulfills your purpose. This means knowing the difference between happiness that's lasting and adds quality to your life and happiness that's superficial. A good way to differentiate the two is by viewing it as experiences and relationships vs. material possessions that you don't need. While buying stuff makes us feel happy in the moment, there are times when we spend it and have buyer's remorse the next day.

When we do things that we really enjoy, that's where we create real and lasting happiness, which is what money at the end of the day is here to provide. While some may say money can't buy happiness, it can if it's used properly. Money can be used to maintain proper health, nurture relationships, and give us greater confidence in ourselves. It can also allow us to enjoy hobbies and gain life enhancing skills. Money can enable you to save and build a cushion so that you're less controlled by it, and that is how money truly buys happiness.

Now that we've touched on exactly what money is, we need to look at it's true purpose and that's where wealth comes in. So, what is wealth? Wealth to me is the side effect of financial literacy. We in society have always been taught that wealth is derived and determined by the size of our paycheck, the things that we own, or how much money is in our bank account. The reality is that everyone's definition of wealth is different when it comes to their own personal life. For some, wealth is a nice car and a beach house, while others find wealth to be a simple and debt-free life. No matter how you look at it, wealth is being able to live the lifestyle you want, but far too often, society impresses upon us that wealth is having the material items. At the end of the day however, material items are just that and while wealth can afford those items, they don't define it for everyone. That's what we often forget when it comes to wealth. For millennials, there have been quite a few studies done as to how we view wealth, and what wealth really means to us.

One survey I found concluded that many people view wealth in the form of experiences such as being able to travel or create new relationships, and that, more than material possessions, seems to be the true meaning of wealth. At the end of the day, what matters most is that we're doing something we're passionate about and something that inspires us. That's also why in the same survey, many millennials said that being in a career that they're passionate about is more important than the salary that they're making[30]. When asked what the most valuable thing is to them, many millennials answered freedom, so while we answer the question of what wealth is correctly, the mindset and execution to achieving it isn't always there.

That's what I'm hoping to convey through his book - the proper execution of how you can use your money as a tool to build your future wealth. Look at Warren Buffett and Jeff Bezos. They are both wealthy beyond imagination, both billionaires, yet they still work hard every day. At 88 years old, Warren Buffet wakes up at 6:45 am every day to start his workday and at 55, Jeff Bezos, the founder of Amazon continues to wake up every day and go to work. Even though they could both retire today and have the most lavish retirements the world has ever seen, neither of them cares to do that because for them it's not about the money, it's about doing something they're passionate about because that's what drives them.

If you're wondering if there is a perfect number for being wealthy, the true answer is no. However, Charles Schwab conducted a modern wealth survey and according to their results, the amount of money to be comfortable today in America at retirement is $1.4 million[31]. So, if you really want to put a number behind wealth, there it is. Now, if you're saying to yourself "I have no idea how that is possible for me", I can show you the basic math that can get to that number if that's what you so choose.

I am going to give an example of a husband and wife, who are both 30 years old and each earning $50,000 a year for a total gross income of $100,000. After we factor in taxes, their net income is reduced to about $78,000 for the year. If they were to invest $1,000 per month into the S&P 500 with an annual rate of return of 8% for 30 years, at the age of 60 that couple would have $1.4 million. That puts them right in line with what according to Charles Schwab's Modern Wealth Survey, is a very comfortable life.

---

[30] Department 26, Millenials and Work

[31] 2019 Modern Wealth Survey, Charles Schwab

Take a look at the graph below to see how investing $1,000 a month for 30 years would earn you just over $1.4 million.

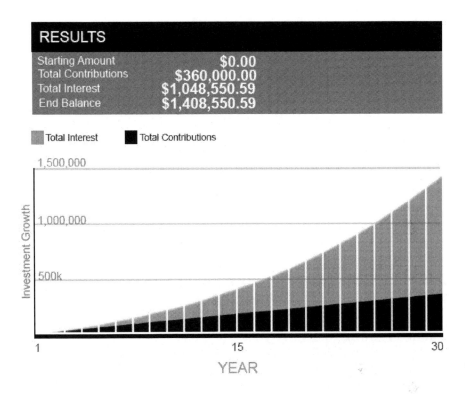

RESULTS	
Starting Amount	$0.00
Total Contributions	$360,000.00
Total Interest	$1,048,550.59
End Balance	$1,408,550.59

Are you able to invest $1,000 a month towards your future? Do you know exactly what you could reasonably invest towards your future at this moment? Do you have an idea of how long you would wish to work? If not, you need to formulate a plan that you can follow to achieve your future goals. An important step is determining your monthly budget and cash flow, which we will discuss in the next chapter.

Many of you are probably thinking that you need to make more money, save more money, or have more money in general and I've had those thoughts too. Many times, I've thought to myself *"If I could just make more money, cut more expenses, or win the lottery I'd have it made."* While it's natural to think this way, doing so only creates more stress around money. When we look at more money as the goal, we will never truly feel satisfied that we have enough, but when money is viewed as a means to an end, we realize that we really can afford anything. Money is everywhere in society, it helps us function daily, and whether you use money to pay your mortgage or to cover your daily expenses, it's an essential part of everyday life. It's not surprising that as a society we constantly focus on money, and unfortunately most of us don't have a healthy relationship with it. We think of money as the enemy, constantly getting in our way because we don't have enough of it. We see money as the ultimate solution to all our problems, when in reality, money is simply the vehicle that takes us to our destination.

In my early 20's I allowed money to control my life and when I first started my career, I focused on using my income to purchase the things I wanted, no matter what they were. I made many reckless purchases that while in the moment felt good, they eventually left me wanting more. At one point, I impulsively purchased a car that I thought would make me happy. I was on cloud nine for a few months after I brought it home, but eventually I hit a point where I began wanting an even nicer car, something bigger and better. I was constantly chasing the idea of having something more because that's what I felt would always keep my happy. I soon came to the realization that I was making purchases without any regard for my future when what I should have been doing was focusing my efforts on investing my hard-earned money in a way that could pay me in the future. Once I realized my mistake, I started to shift my focus from the material things making me happy, to investing in a secure financial future. This is why defining your future goals is important, so you don't lose track and spend your money unwisely.

For every new millennial client that I work with, I ask them if they were to get $1,000,000 next week, how would they spend it all. Then I ask them out of all the ways they would spend it, which of those ways would help sustain them in the future. I ask this question because people tend to think in the now, rather than how they can invest in ways to pay themselves in the future. The point of this exercise is to help them clear their mind of the material items and instant gratifications that clutter their mind when they think about money. This exercise also shows what millennials do as they earn their paycheck, they focus on the now but not on the future.

The challenge we face is wrapping our minds around the concept of needing more money. Social media and today's society have helped to create a mindset for instant gratification. This can lead to our demise if we're only focusing on the shiny objects in the present and not on the things that will pay us in the future. One day we will all reach a point that we're no longer able to support ourselves by working for a paycheck, so we need to have another form of income in place.

Money is not the enemy and should not be feared, especially when it comes to your current financial situation. If you're afraid of money, you may try to avoid it by not tracking your spending or avoiding the creation and use of a budget. When you avoid managing your financial situation because you think it's impossible, you aren't using the right mindset. It's always important to take control of your finances no matter how uncomfortable it may be at first.

Money management starts with a meaningful goal. Do you want to stop living paycheck to paycheck by better allocating your money every week or pay down your debt, so it no longer restricts you from enjoying life? No matter how you want to use money, knowing the end goal is how you can come up with a strategy to reach that goal. If you want to increase the amount of money that you have, you can begin by earning more, saving more, and investing more. When my own mindset shifted, I realized that earning more money and investing money into things that would pay me in the future were crucial methods to reach my goal of financial freedom. You should strive to maintain this same mindset and focus on securing your future rather than just spending money on your immediate pleasures.

Sometimes it's easier to focus on securing your future when you break up your goals into smaller milestones, so they aren't overwhelming. For instance, if you have $38,000 worth of student loan debt, don't think about your payoff in terms of months or years, instead think of it in bite size chunks. Paying $50 a week towards your debt is a lot more realistic than worrying how you'll pay down $38,000. When you're focused on action, you're more likely to take the right steps and feel in control. This makes it much easier to view money as a tool rather than a daunting milestone.

I know you might be thinking that all this sure is easy to say when you're not struggling to make ends meet each month, and you're right. But for me, specific and meaningful goals are what motivated me and shifted my mindset to no longer focus on having more money just to spend it. I'd argue that meaningful goals are even more important when you're struggling with money because it's so overwhelming. When you don't know where to start, it's much easier to just give up and continue putting your entire life on a credit card.

A well-known economist once said, *"how strange it is that we live in the richest society in human history, yet we don't teach our children how we got to be the richest society in human history"*. I think he nailed it on both counts. As a society, we are unbelievably wealthy but it's strange that we don't give much thought on how to create that wealth. That's what this book is about - to educate you on each small effort that it takes to build up your wealth and make a difference in your own life.

I believe that wealth shows up in a few ways – through an abundance of time, through an abundance of money, and through an abundance of health and happiness. The problem is that we often sacrifice one form of wealth for another, like when we work long hours and deprive ourselves of proper self-care and a social life in order to make more money in our paycheck. That's an important psychological aspect that you need to learn before you start building wealth or getting yourself out of debt and into a more prosperous future.

For many of us, becoming wealthy is a journey and there will always be some that have it happen sooner than others. But when it comes to money, remember that if you don't understand its purpose, you can easily lose it. That's why a large percentage of lottery winners end up losing the money that they win and often end up in a mountain of debt. It's crazy to think that someone can potentially win millions of dollars and end up with millions of dollars of debt, but it does happen and it's all because of choices. If you make poor choices with your money and squander it, you're left with nothing.

A man named Jim Hayes won $19 million in a lottery jackpot and he took that money and spent it carelessly on multiple homes and even purchased an entire collection of every Lamborghini ever produced. He would go on extravagant gambling trips to Vegas and travel all over the world, until one day he woke up in a massive amount of debt. As his houses were being foreclosed upon and his cars were repossessed, he found himself living out of a garage and began robbing banks just to survive, landing him a spot on the FBI's most wanted list. Not only did he have a poor understanding of how to spend money, but he had an even worse understanding of how to obtain it. He was eventually caught and sentenced to quite a few years in prison. Trust me, you don't ever want to end up like Jim.

That brings me to another important aspect of being wealthy. Most wealthy people don't have extravagant material items such as the large house or a collection of sports cars. Being wealthy isn't always about the same material things because its definition can vary from person to person. Some people use their wealth to buy a house they love, and they spend time and money renovating it until they have their perfect home. Others enjoy using their wealth to travel the world and see new places. And for some, being wealthy is just living a simple life, where they can afford food and schooling for their children and enjoy their financial freedom. The American dream isn't to be rich, it's to be free. Creating your wealth creates your freedom in life. Chasing money and riches doesn't make you free.

No matter what your own vision of wealth looks like, remember that it doesn't happen overnight. Your vision of wealth may be very different from someone else's and that's okay. And while we do need money, we shouldn't abandon our own happiness just to gain it. At its core, though, money can be a powerful tool when used the right way. A simple shift in mindset isn't going to change your financial situation overnight, but it's a necessary step in getting control of your finances and building wealth for the future. Moving forward, I want to discuss how to implement the proper mindset with money so that you can structure your own future by setting realistic goals, creating a budget, and working towards financial freedom. Most importantly, I want to talk about how you can begin to secure that future by consistently saving and contributing into the right areas that will one day pay you back when you no longer want to work for a paycheck

Now that we've covered all the challenges we're facing, the lack of education that has made these challenges even greater, and the scams that prey upon our hopes and desires to build our wealth, I want to shift our focus to how we can create a solid financial plan. A solid financial plan is like building a home.

The most critical part to any home is its foundation. Without a strong and solid foundation, the house can come crashing down. The foundation of your financial plan is your current net worth. If you don't know what you have or what you owe, you cannot move beyond that point. If you attempt to, you could have issues arise in the future.

The next stage of building your financial plan is framing out the first floor. When you come home from work, you enter through the front door and when you leave for work, you exit through that same door. In your financial plan, the front door on your first floor represents the money coming in through your paycheck and going out in the form of expenses. The first floor of your financial plan is focused on managing your cash flow.

Next you need to build the second floor of your financial home. When you have a second-floor bedroom, you walk up the steps to your bedroom where you rest. You wake up the next day well-rested and you go down the steps and out the front door to work. In your financial plan, your money will go upstairs to rest and grow for the future through the form of investments, so one day it can come down the steps acting as your cash flow with some going out the front door to cover your expenses.

The last and most critical piece of any home is the roof, protecting you from the elements and the unknown. Just like with a house, your financial plan must have protections for your life, whether it's in the form of life insurance, disability insurance, or estate documents. Your job moving forward is to begin building your financial plan.

Exercise 1:
Determine Your Current Net Worth

Assets – Liabilities = Net Worth

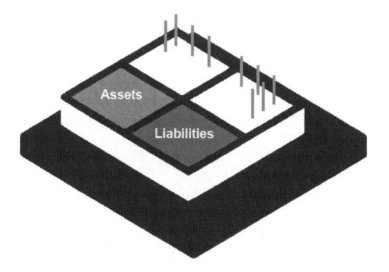

I want to help you determine your current net worth. Your current net worth is everything you currently own (your assets) minus the current debts that you owe (your liabilities). Assets include cash, investments, your home or other real estate, cars, and anything else of value. Liabilities are what you owe on those assets such as car loans, mortgages, and debt from credit cards or student loans. Take a piece of paper and make two columns.

In the first column I want you to list the value of all your assets including your home, your car, the current balances of your checking and savings accounts, any retirement accounts through your employer, any additional investment accounts, and any objects of value such as collectibles.

In the second column I want you to list all your outstanding liabilities like the balance on your mortgage, balance on any car loans, outstanding credit card balances, student loans, personal loans, and any other outstanding debt obligations.

Now I need you to total both columns and subtract your total liabilities from your total assets. This number represents your current net worth. Your net worth represents the foundation of your financial plan.

The average net worth of Americans under age 35 is $6,676. For Americans 35-44 the average net worth is $35,000.

Don't feel bad if your net worth isn't where you'd like it to be. It's never too late to get your financial house in order. Just remember to start today instead of tomorrow!

"The person who doesn't know where their next dollar is coming from usually doesn't know where their last dollar went."

Unknown

Chapter 6

Money In, Money Out

When it comes to income, many of us will claim that we don't make enough to get by each month and we're stuck living paycheck to paycheck. But 90% of our money problems don't necessarily have anything to do with how much we make, but rather how we use the money we make. That's why before you even begin to plan for your future, you need to understand your current financial situation and be able to control and track your spending. That's where a budget comes into play because it allows you to assign a job to every dollar that you earn and enables you to track if that money is going where it should be.

Even though you might earn $50,000 a year, you aren't bringing that amount home because taxes get taken out before it even hits your bank account. Taxes and deductions are important to understand, as they affect what your take-home, or net income is. Portions of your paycheck are deducted every pay period and they're listed as withholdings on your paystub because they are literally withheld from your paycheck. Your gross earnings are what you start out with, but that amount decreases as deductions are taken out. Federal, state, and local income tax are all automatically deducted as well as a mandatory payroll deduction for FICA, the Federal Insurance Contributions Act. This tax is taken out to pay older Americans their social security retirement benefits and Medicare or hospital insurance benefits. Some tax withholdings are benefiting others that are retired while other tax withholdings ensure that federal, state, and local governments function properly by maintaining roads, overseeing parks, ensuring the operation of police departments, and funding public schools. Your net pay is what you're left with after these deductions are taken out and your budget should always be based off your net income.

Speaking of taxes, you know that saying that nothing in life is certain but death and taxes? Well, it's more like nothing in life is certain but death and overpaying your taxes. That's right, if you receive a refund check from the Internal Revenue Service (IRS) after you file your taxes each year, you're overpaying and that's why the government is giving it back to you. Income tax differs from many of the other taxes because the money we pay towards it never even hits our bank account and is taken directly from our paycheck. When you get a tax return from the government, they are simply handing you back your own hard-earned money from earlier in the year. Many people look forward to a tax return and they see it as free money, when in reality it's just an interest free loan you gave the government.

If you made $20 and you gave me $5 of your earnings to hold on to, then I turned around and gave it back to you at the end of the year, would you be excited? Probably not, because there really was no point in letting me hold that money. That's the same concept with a tax return. You basically lent the government your money to hold for an entire year without earning any interest on it like you would if you put that money into a savings or investment fund. What most people don't realize is that while the government holds onto your money, they lend it out for other projects and earn a return on it. A refund of $3,000 means that you as the taxpayer could have been receiving an extra $250 in pay each month[32], which can mean the difference between making a debt payment on time or additional savings toward your future. Even if you have every intention of using your tax refund money each year to pay towards debt, build your savings fund, or even invest, most people end up using it on a once-per-year splurge.

So, what should you do to avoid overpaying the IRS each year and giving Uncle Sam an interest free loan? Simply adjust your withholdings. The goal is to get the amount you withhold as close to your yearly tax bill as possible. If you have too little taken out, you'll owe money at tax time so it's a good idea to use the withholding calculator on the IRS website to fill in your information and see what the ideal withholding amount is for you. You can change the amount you withhold on a new W-4 that you file with

---

[32] National Foundation for Credit Counseling Survey, 2014

70

your employer. If you previously were overpaying on your taxes, the extra amount you'll bring home each month can be a great increase in your monthly budget. Now that you understand how to maximize your net income each month, it's time to talk about how to budget that income.

Budgeting is the process of creating a plan to assign each dollar you earn a job of either spending, saving, or investing. Creating a budget allows you to determine in advance whether you will have enough money to take care of necessities and purchase the things you enjoy. Budgeting allows you to create a spending plan for your money and ensures you will have enough money for the important things you need first like a roof over your head, utilities, a form of transportation, and groceries. Following a budget will also keep you out of debt by ensuring you allocate your money to the important things and can prevent you from using a credit card to cover an unexpected expense. Budgeting can help you work your way out of debt because you can see how much more you can pay towards the minimum on any outstanding credit card balances you carry.

After creating your initial budget, don't be surprised if you find it necessary to make adjustments over the next few months. It may take some time to get your spending on track and identify expenses you can reduce or eliminate all together. A good way to start is by making a monthly budget that includes your necessities and spending money for things that are important to you. As my good friend, Ellen Ross mentions in her book, *Fixing Your Finances*, setting money aside for things like vet bills for your pets or maintenance costs for your vehicle is crucial so that when the expense comes up, you don't have to go into debt or take money from your savings to cover it.

Extending your budget out into the future like this also allows you to forecast how much money you can save towards important things like a family vacation, a new car, or household repairs. By realistically budgeting to forecast your spending for the year, it can also help with long-term financial planning. Based on your income, you can determine how much to put aside for saving and investing.

The most important thing when it comes to budgeting is that it will only work if you commit to using it, so you need to prioritize following your budget each month. Say you set $50 aside every month for dining out and it's only the middle of the month when a friend asks you to meet up for dinner and drinks. The problem is that you've already used up your $50 allowance for dining out so now you need to make a smart financial choice. Are you going to charge it on your credit card and go into more debt? Are you going to take money out of another budget category that you've been saving for and risk not having enough in the future for that expense? Or are you going to ask your friends if they can just come over to your house for some drinks and you'll grill up the burgers you have in your freezer? You can still benefit from the company, but not at the expense of throwing off your budget for the month.

After the first few months of using a budget, you'll notice that it gets easier to think before you purchase something. It's also important that once your paycheck hits your bank account, you follow your budget, otherwise you'll be impulsively spending that money before you even use it for the necessities like mortgage or rent, utilities, and groceries. Budgeting also makes you consider if you're spending your hard-earned money in the best way possible. Rather than using Uber Eats to deliver a $10 meal to your door for $20, drive up the road and pick up your order yourself. You may slip up in the beginning as you get used to budgeting your money, but don't beat yourself up over it. Smart people learn from their mistakes, and even smarter people learn from the mistakes of others.

Take MC Hammer for example, who once had a net worth of about $33 million before he declared bankruptcy in 1996. He had $30 million in unpaid debts because he never tracked his finances and was too caught up in his own lavish lifestyle and extravagant spending habits to notice how quickly he was burning through his money.

There's a common misconception out there that only poor people have a budget, which just isn't true. A budget has nothing to do with how much you make but has everything to do with directing your income and controlling your spending. Wealthy people use a budget to determine where their money will go each month so that they don't end up spending too much in one category when it could be used in a more beneficial way like investing. Having more money does not solve your problems but having a budget can. It's your money and you need to have control over it instead of letting your money control you.

An important category to include in your budget is the amount you put into savings so that you can ensure you're actively putting money away monthly, whether it's $5 or $500. Too many people focus on the fact that they only make a certain amount of income each month and they live paycheck to paycheck, so they don't bother to set even a tiny amount aside for savings. Each month they pay their necessities and purchase things they want, but don't necessarily need, until their bank account reaches $0 and they have no positive cash flow left over to save or invest.

This is what I call the rat race, where you're not getting ahead but just repeating the same cycle over and over each month. If you want to stop living paycheck to paycheck, you need to break this cycle and evaluate your spending to see what expenses can be reduced or eliminated altogether. You can do this by cutting the cord on cable if you find you never watch TV anymore, using coupons on groceries, or doing simple car or home maintenance yourself instead of paying someone else to do it. If there are things you spend money on each month simply for the convenience, ask yourself if the price of convenience is worth it.

For those that have a lower monthly income and can't possibly cut costs any further, it's often a sign that they need to increase their income. This can be done in several ways such as asking for a raise, applying for a higher paying job, or looking into a side hustle.

A side hustle can be a part time job or something that you're passionate about that you could do on the side but isn't as time consuming as a full-time job. A side hustle allows you to create an additional stream of income to help pay down your debts, set money aside for savings, or invest money in areas that will generate an even larger paycheck for you in the future. Whatever your financial goal is, I think it's crucial that you consider a side hustle as a way for you to fast track achieving your goals.

To get started with a side hustle, think of something you're passionate about and good at and determine if there is a way for you to monetize it. There's a great book by bestselling author Tony Whatley called *Side Hustle Millionaire*. It's a great resource to get you started if you are considering creating a side hustle. Some people have even created side hustles that become their full-time career.

If you want to get ahead, you must take action, even if that means sacrificing some of your free time on the weekends to take on extra shifts. If this is the case, try to keep a positive outlook by telling yourself that this is only temporary, and you won't have to work two jobs forever if you hustle as hard as you can to get ahead and pay off your debt or build up your savings fund sooner. Everyone struggles with money at times, but it's not the struggle that defines us, it's how we overcome the struggle. It may not be the most pleasant time in your life, but it will pay off in the future.

When I was in my 20's, I just wanted to make money and spend it on things that made me happy in the moment without having to make any sacrifices. Eventually I realized that living my life this way was costing me a secure financial future and I began to prioritize making sacrifices when it was necessary, so I could save and invest more money. You can't just live for today, you must always consider your future, even if that comes in the form of sacrificing your need for instant gratification.

So how do you make a budget? First, start by making a list of your current net income every month and your current monthly expenses. You want to make sure you include as many categories as possible in your budget for things like gas, public transportation, childcare, entertainment like dining out, gym memberships, subscriptions, and anything else you can think of that you regularly spend money on. You can break those expenses into categories like groceries, fun, utilities, car maintenance, and household repairs. For yearly or quarterly expenses, divide the average yearly cost by 12 so you can determine out how much you should set aside each month towards that expense.

A great way to identify exactly what you spend money on and how much you spend, is by going over your receipts, credit card statements, and bank account activity. Even if you notice that you've been spending money on things you don't necessarily need, it's important to include those costs in your budget at first so you can see how much you're currently spending. If you aren't already, consider using an Excel or Google Spreadsheet for your budget and input the budget categories and expense amounts. When you're all done, take a long hard look at what number is left once you subtract your monthly spending from your monthly income. If it's not a positive number, it's time to make some changes.

This is where you cut down the amounts you spend on both your needs and your wants. Everyone needs to buy themselves clothing occasionally but spending hundreds of dollars on an excessive number of shoes is a habit that can be changed. A good rule of thumb is that if you don't have money to buy something with cash at the time twice over, you can't afford it. You should now have a good idea of how you've been spending your money each month and how you plan to start spending it in the future. The golden rule will always be to make sure your income is higher than your expenses to give yourself a positive cash flow. That positive cash flow is what allows you to make progress on your goals like paying down your debt, building up your savings, and investing to make money for your future.

The next thing you need to do is come up with a way to track your expenses as they happen. Some people use an app, some prefer using a spreadsheet, others prefer using paper. Every time you spend money, you must track the date, the expense type, and how much you spend. I recommend doing this weekly so it's easier to track and keep up with because it you do it monthly, you may feel overwhelmed and it will discourage you from tracking anything at all. The whole point of tracking your spending is to help you understand where your money is going and if you're following your budget or not. You can also identify and categorize what you should allow more money for each month. I recommend using your debit card for much of your spending until your budget is under control, so you can easily track your purchases. Spending cash is a lot harder to track especially if you don't save your receipts. Make it a priority each week to set aside time for tracking that week's expenses.

You should also automate your savings by having as much as you can each month transferred into your savings or investments, so you can guarantee you're setting money aside for a specific goal you've set for yourself. Automate as much as possible so the money you've allocated for a specific purpose gets there with minimal effort on your part. It's a simple way to ensure that you're holding yourself accountable with minimal effort. When you make it easier for yourself to save money, you will have a better sense of control and confidence over your finances.

In your budget you should spend no more than 50% of your after-tax dollars or net income, on necessities, no more than 30% on wants, and at least 20% on savings and debt repayment. For necessities, 50% of your net income should be going towards things like groceries, housing, basic utilities, transportation, insurance, minimum loan payments (anything beyond the minimum goes into the savings and debt repayment category), and child care or other expenses you need to live. If your necessities are less than the 50% limit, investing the excess into areas that will pay you in the future is smart. Ideally, you should consider keeping your needs under 50%. This is the case for my wife and I as we live a relatively frugal life except for our love of cars. We live in a modest town home, maintain our budget, and keep our needs below 50% of our net income, which then allows us to allocate more towards investments.

You should leave 30% of your income set aside for wants. Separating wants from needs can be difficult but remember that needs are essential for you to live and work while wants aren't crucial to your survival. Typical wants include dining out, buying gifts, vacations, sports cars, and entertainment. It's not always easy to decide if something like a gym membership or organic groceries is a want or need, but that's when you need to start making sacrifices. If you're attempting to get out of debt as soon as possible, you may decide that your wants can wait until you have your debt under control. According to a CNBC report in 2018, people are spending an average of $450 a month on impulse purchases for things they don't need[33]. It's critical to follow the 30% rule for your wants so that you avoid being part of that statistic.

Every budget needs wiggle room — maybe you forgot about an expense or one was bigger than you anticipated — as well as some money you're entitled to spend as you wish. Your budget is a tool to help you, not a straitjacket to restrict you from enjoying life. If there's no money for fun, you'll be less likely to stick with your budget. Many of my peers are just beginning to make good money and many of them aren't spending it wisely. It's unfortunate because I know they're smart and they know what they're supposed to be doing, but they just keep spending and spending without putting money towards any sort of investments for the future. Are you

---

[33] CNBC.com Article by Sarah O'Brien, 2018

willing to cut down on spending money excessively so that you can have a better future?

Finally, you should commit 20% of your income to savings, paying off your debt, and investing in your future. Make sure you think of the bigger financial picture with this as it may mean two-stepping between saving and debt repayment to accomplish your most pressing goals. My wife and I make it a priority to save and invest closer to 30% of our income each month. Sadly, most people, especially those that are younger, have this number closer to 0%. Sometimes people can be so focused on paying off their debt that they forget to save or invest for their future paycheck. I think this is a mistake because it's very difficult to suddenly begin aggressively saving for your future. That's why you should get into the habit of investing for your future as soon as possible, even if it's just $5 a day.

The 50-30-20 budget plan is simple and easy follow. The average American makes $27 an hour[34]. If you save 2 hours of your day's pay, $50 a day and invest that money for the next 20 years with an assumed annual rate of return of 8%, you'll have $858,990 at the end of 20 years. If you do this for 30 years with an assumed annual rate of return of 8% you'll have $2,126,419 at the end of 30 years. This all by investing just $50 a day from your pay! I like the simplicity of this 50-30-20 plan because if you follow these guidelines over the long term, you can have manageable debt, room to indulge on occasion, and a savings to pay irregular or unexpected expenses and retire comfortably.

It may be helpful for you to consider breaking the different aspects of your budget into 6 different priorities:

Priority 1: Start Your Emergency Fund
Many experts recommend building up several months' worth of bare-bones living expenses. I suggest starting with an emergency fund of at least $500 which should be enough to cover small emergencies and repairs, and then you can build your emergency fund up from there. If you can get an emergency fund of at least $500 in place, you're ahead of most Americans already!

---

[34] Bureau of Labor Statistics, 2019

Remember, you can't get out of debt without a way to avoid more debt when something unexpected happens and you'll sleep better knowing you have a financial cushion.

Priority 2: Getting the Employer Match on Your Tax Advantaged Accounts

If your employer offers a match on your tax-advantaged accounts, take advantage of it and get that easy money first. For most people, that means a 401(k) and if your employer offers a match, make sure you contribute at least enough to grab the maximum match. This is free money so take advantage of it! You should make this a priority over your debts because you won't get another chance this big at free money, tax breaks, and compound interest. Ultimately, you have a better shot at building wealth by getting in the habit of regular long-term savings. Every $1,000 you don't put away in your 20's could be $20,000 less that you have at retirement!

Priority 3: Get Rid of Toxic Debt

Once you've hit your 401k and match, if available, go after the toxic debt in your life like high-interest credit card debt, personal loans, and rent-to-own payments. These debts carry interest rates so high that you end up repaying two or three times what you originally borrowed.

Priority 4: Save for Your Retirement

Once you've knocked off any toxic debt, the next task is to get yourself on track for retirement. Aim to save 20% of your gross income which includes your company match if there is one. In the coming chapters, we will dive further into retirement funds and investing to help you determine the right areas for you to invest.

Priority 5: Debt Repayment

These are payments beyond the minimum each month so that you can pay off the remaining debt. If you've already paid off your most toxic debt, what's left is probably a lower interest rate and often tax-deductible like a mortgage. You should tackle these debts only after you've gotten your other financial priorities accomplished. Any wiggle room you have here comes from the money available for wants in your budget or from saving money on necessities. You should never use money from your emergency fund or retirement to pay off your debt.

Priority 6: Celebrate Your Hard Work

Congratulations on getting your financial priorities accomplished! You have a working budget, a healthy emergency fund, you've paid off toxic debt, and you're socking 20% away towards a retirement nest egg that will serve as your paycheck when you no longer wish to work. You've built a habit of saving that gives you immense financial flexibility. If you've reached this point, consider saving for irregular expenses that aren't emergencies such as a new roof or your next car. Those expenses will come no matter what, and it's better to save before you need them than borrow when you're unprepared.

As millennials, we seem to have problems with our spending and struggle with staying out of debt. A budget can guide us to make better spending choices with the way we use our hard-earned money, but when it comes to debt, you must work as hard as possible to pay it off. You have likely heard all sorts of advice on how to handle debt – some say to start with the highest interest rate, some say start with the smallest balance, and some tell you that you it's good to consolidate your debt. The way you handle paying off your debt is based on your own personal situation but there is one aspect of paying off debt that I want to discuss.

There's always been a debate about whether the debt snowball or the debt avalanche is a better method to pay off debt. The debt snowball method, made popular by Dave Ramsey, involves paying the minimum monthly payment on all your debts and then using any leftover money to pay down the smallest debt first. Once that debt is paid off you move on to the next smallest debt. Once you pay off your smallest debt, usually in a matter of months, you get a small win up front. By the time you work way up to the largest debt, you'll have a huge amount of money to throw towards your remaining debt each month. This method can make a large student loan debt or mortgage balance seem less intimidating. The downside to this method is that the interest rates on your large balances are still working against you as you focus on your smaller debts.

The debt avalanche method is like the debt snowball in that you make the minimum payment on all your debts. As you pay off each debt, that minimum payment gets added to the monthly payment for the next debt, and by the time you get to your last debt you are throwing large amounts of money at it. Where it differs is that the order you pay your debts off goes by the interest rate rather than the balance. The highest interest rate debt gets focused on first and you work your way down to the lowest interest rate debt. The math is better with the debt avalanche and you will save some money in the long run using this method.

While the avalanche method saves you money in interest in the long run, it could be harder to follow for some that are in a tough financial spot and can barely make ends meet. Sometimes just the idea of focusing on one debt a bit more than others, whether it's the smallest debt, or the one with the highest interest, can keep you on the right track. For others, remembering that you're saving money in the long run can keep you focused on eliminating your largest debt. As you pay off your debt and free up your cash flow, you can then avalanche that money for saving and investing just as you have done for paying down your debt.

Remember that the benefits of taking the time to create and follow a budget are crucial to building a better future for yourself and resolving any current financial struggles you have. By taking the time to plan things out, you can evaluate your current situation, identify any overspending, close leaks in your savings, and identify ways you can invest in your future. If you don't take the time to do all these things, you can end up working until you're 70, still living paycheck to paycheck, and still carrying around a mountain of debt on your shoulders. It takes time to learn positive budgeting habits, but you must start somewhere. Many times, people will find that their spending and other financial behaviors improve as they begin to think about investments and long-term financial planning. As millennials, we have time on our side so it's never too late to start budgeting and take back control of our money. Speaking of debt, it's time that we discuss debt in more detail and even a few ways that debt can be your best friend if you use it wisely.

Exercise 2:
Creating Your Budget

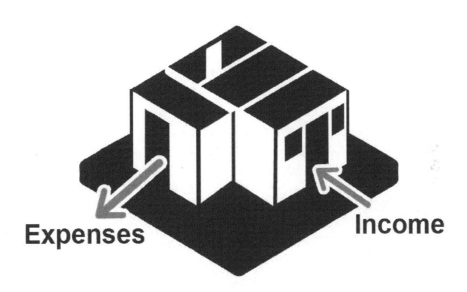

Expenses   **Income**

Use the information from this chapter to build the first floor of your house for your financial plan and create your budget to evaluate your cash flow. It's important that you know how much money is coming into your house in the form of your net income and leaving your house in the form of expenses.

Determine your monthly net income by adding up what you take home from all your income sources including your full-time job and any side hustles. Enter that amount below.

Net Income: _____

Now you need to determine the cash flow that leaves your house in the form of expenses. Make 3 columns, one for necessities, one for wants, and one for debt repayment, savings, and investments.

Next you must figure out the percentage each column represents of your total net income.

For each column, take the total and divide it by your monthly net income, then multiply that number by 100. This will be your percentage of your budget that goes to each one of those areas.

% of net income for necessities: _____
% of net income for wants: _____
% of net income for debt, savings, and investing: _____

Remember the 50-30-20 rule. If you are spending over 50% on your necessities, over 30% on your wants, or allocating less than 20% towards your debt, savings, and investing column, review these categories in your monthly budget.

Make a list of action items below (reduce or eliminate your cable bill, set up automatic transfers to your savings, etc.) and start working on those immediately.

"Today, there are three kinds of people: the have's, the have-not's, and the have-not-paid-for-what-they-haves."

Earl Wilson

Chapter 7

Your Best Friend, Debt

Now that you have a better understanding of how to budget your money, it's time to focus on debt. Debt comes in many shapes and sizes, but when used properly, it can be your best friend. In this chapter we will talk about how financially independent people use debt to build their wealth.

According to a poll from Money After Graduation, over 60% of millennials carry credit card and student loan debt, over 30% of millennials have a car loan, and just over 20% have a line of credit[35]. It's clear that most millennials carry some type of debt and while many people advise you to never use debt at all, it's important to understand the difference between good debt and bad debt. While it's possible to live debt-free, using debt to your benefit can really pay off. Very few people earn enough money to pay cash for life's most important purchases such as a home or car, and that's why you need to consider if the debt you're taking on is good or bad.

There are a few things you need to understand about credit and debt. Just because most American's do something does not mean it's a good idea. Americans have more debt than ever and the numbers I'm about to share should scare the crap out of you like they do me. 80% of Americans live in debt[36], with the average American household having over $9,000 worth of high interest credit card debt and we, as a society are becoming more and more reliant on debt every single day[37]. Americans now have over 1

---

[35] Moneyaftergraduation.com

[36] Nitro College, 2019

[37] ValuePenguin, June 2019

trillion (yes, a 1 with nine 0's after it) dollars in credit card debt, housing, auto loans, and other types of debt[38].

It's important that you understand that you can get paid to be different from most Americans. Most Americans get a bill from their lenders saying how much money they owe in interest at the end of each month. On the other hand, you have some people that don't get a bill and instead receive a check or other perks from the credit card companies because they never carry a balance. You see, credit card companies understand that if they offer perks like 1 or 2% cashback, 9 out of 10 people will take advantage of this opportunity. Here's how to really win in this situation. If, and only if, you can control your spending, only buy things that you can afford, and can commit to paying off your entire balance every month, then you can get paid for your regular spending. If you're wondering how you can afford something, just remember the rule of 2. If you can't buy 2 of them, you can't afford 1 of them. If you cannot control your spending, then don't use your credit cards and pay with cash.

The credit score system is one big game where you have more losers than winners. Did you know you can have a great credit score while paying off your credit card balance every single month? Your credit score is a number that rates how good you are at debt and then ultimately allows you to get access to more debt. Credit bureaus and lending agencies are making billions because they've created a game out of helping people buy things they can't afford. Ever wish there was an investment that would generate a 10% return on your money every single year? Well, it's possible and I can show you someone who's getting not just a 10% annual return but a 25% annual return on their money every year, the credit card companies.

So, what is your credit score and how is it calculated? Think of your credit score as your financial Grade Point Average (GPA). Banks, lenders, and other entities will review your score to help them determine whether to approve you for a loan, credit, and sometimes even employment. Your credit score is a three-digit number generated by a mathematical algorithm that uses information from your credit report. This score is designed to predict risk, specifically the likelihood that you will become seriously delinquent on your credit obligations in the 24 months after scoring.

---

[38] Payments Journal, November 2018

Data from your credit report goes into five major categories that make up a FICO score. The scoring model weighs some factors more heavily than others, such as payment history and debt owed. Here are the five biggest things that affect your score, how they affect your credit, and what it means when you apply for a loan.

Payment History: 35%: There is one question lenders have on their minds when they give someone money, *"Will I get it back?"* The most important component of your credit score looks at how well you can be trusted to repay funds that are loaned to you.

Amounts Owed: 30%: You currently make all your payments on time, but what if you're about to reach a breaking point? This is a look at your credit utilization ratio. This is a measure of how much debt you have compared to your available credit limits. This is the second-most important component in your credit score.

Length of Credit History: 15%: Your credit score also considers how long you have been using credit. A long credit history is helpful, but a short history can be fine too if you've made your payments on time and don't owe too much. Many personal finance experts always recommend leaving credit card accounts open, even if you cut them up and don't use them anymore. The account's age by itself will help boost your score. If you close your oldest account, you could see your overall score decline.

New Credit: 10%: Your FICO score considers how many new accounts you have. It will look at how many new accounts you have applied for recently as well as the last time you opened a new account.

Types of Credit in Use: 10%: The final piece to the FICO formula is the mix of different types of credit, such as credit cards, store accounts, personal loans, and mortgages. It also looks at how many total accounts you have.

Now let's look at the way banks work when it comes to your money. When you put your money into a checking or savings account at a bank, the bank doesn't just sock it away in an underground vault. Instead it lends your money to other individuals or companies that need it. Thanks to the magic of fractional banking, when your bank lends your money to other people, the bank is creating money and a profit for itself. Whenever you take on debt, whether it's good or bad, the banks make money. Our modern banking system only requires that banks keep a small fraction of the funds deposited with them so there is money available if people choose to withdraw it.

Banks borrow funds from their depositors (those who put money into checking or savings accounts) and in turn lend much of those funds to the banks' borrowers (those in need of funds such as a mortgage). Banks make money this way by charging borrowers a higher percentage interest rate for a loan than what is paid to depositors for the use of their money. This practice of fractional lending gives banks the ability to "create" money. For instance, if you deposit $100,000 at the bank and the bank has a reserve requirement of 10%, that means they must keep $10,000 of your money on reserve and can lend out the other $90,000. The bank has taken $100,000 and has turned it into $190,000 by giving you a $100,000 credit on your deposits and then lending the additional $90,000 out to someone else.

Now, if you take this out a little further, you will see that your original $100,000 can become a much larger amount by the time it's all over. Here's how:

	Deposits	10% Reserve Requirement	Bank loans out
You	$100,000	$10,000	$90,000
Person 2	$90,000	$9,000	$81,000
Person 3	$81,000	$8,100	$72,900
Person 4	$72,900	$7,290	$65,610
Person 5	$65,610	$6,561	$59.049
Person 6	$59,049	$5,905	$53,144
Person 7...	$53,144...	$5,314...	$47,830...

This chart can go on and on, ultimately the bank can grow your initial $100,000 into $1,000,000 with a 10% reserve requirement.

No matter how you use it, debt is debt and it always comes with a risk. The difference between good and bad debt is that good debt has the potential to increase your net worth and generate financial gain, while bad debt involves borrowing money to purchase assets that depreciate and lose their value over time. Good debt is debt that can be written off with taxes or has an interest rate under 6%. Determining whether a debt is good or bad often depends on an individual's financial situation but if it won't go up in value or generate an income for you in the future, it's generally a bad debt.

To understand bad debt, think about things you borrow money for that won't give you any sort of return while you carry that debt. It's important to note that any debt that has an interest rate of 10% or more is definitely bad debt. For example, if you borrow $10,000 at 10% interest, it will cost you $1,000 a year to borrow. If you plan to pay that $10,000 off within a year, you'll have paid $11,000 total. But if you choose to pay that debt off over the course of 5 or even 10 years, the additional amount you owe gets higher and higher. There aren't many investments out there that will give you double digit returns to begin with and virtually none that do so consistently, so it's never a good idea to borrow money at a double-digit interest rate. By the way, most credit cards have an interest rate higher than 10%, so keep that in mind any time you think about signing up for one and using it on a purchase you can't afford in cash.

One example of bad debt is something that almost everyone has, a car. Most cars will depreciate over time and won't make us a profit when we sell it since the value will inevitably be less than when we first purchased it. When you purchase a car, you pay money during the life of the vehicle to maintain it and keep it running all while it decreases in value. This is what makes buying a pre-owned vehicle a better choice than buying a brand-new one. With a pre-owned vehicle, someone already took a hit on the initial drop in value when they drove the new car off the lot. Borrowing to buy a quickly-depreciating asset such as a brand-new car, especially if your current vehicle is roadworthy, is a good example of bad debt and here's why. Say your new car costs $35,000. With a 10% down payment and 3.5% interest on a 5-year loan, the total cost of that car, including financing, is almost $38,000. But after owning that car for four years, its value might fall to about $15,000 and you'll still have another year left to pay off the loan you took out for it. There was no financial gain here for you.

When used irresponsibly, credit cards are another form of bad debt. This is because when you charge something to your credit card and don't pay it off in full after the current billing cycle, the lender charges you interest every month on that balance. Most credit cards charge interest rates of over 20%, which is why credit cards are dangerous if you're not paying them off. When you use your credit card to go on a shopping spree for new clothes or to buy the newest laptop model and you aren't paying it off in full on your next bill, you're carrying bad debt. As Americans, we seem to be obsessed with poor credit card usage and our spending has reached new heights. 74 million Americans now have more credit card debt than they have money in their emergency savings, which is the highest level in 9 years[39]! That's why it's so important to understand the difference between good and bad debt, especially when it comes to credit cards. When you're going into debt with credit cards that have interest rates well over 20%, this is a form of toxic debt and you should avoid getting into this situation as much as possible. If you're actively paying down your credit card debt and are afraid you'll use your credit card for impulse purchases, leave it at home.

A way credit cards can offer a benefit when used correctly, is with balance transfers. Let's assume that a credit card company offers a 0% interest rate for 18 months with a 2% balance transfer fee. This means that you can transfer your current balance on your existing card that has a high interest rate to the new card and pay it off while it accrues 0% interest. Let's say you have a credit card with a $4,000 balance and you're paying 20% interest. You can transfer to the new credit card and pay 0% interest for the first 18 months. The cost for transferring your balance to the new card is 2% which means you must pay $80 to get the ability to pay off the balance in 18 months with no added interest.

If you have successfully paid down your credit card debt and want to use your cards to keep your credit score healthy, you can charge recurring expenses that you already budget for, like groceries, and pay off the balance in full after your billing cycle ends. When you have your spending under control, successfully

---

[39] Bankrate survey, February 2019

follow a budget every month, and understand the right way to use a credit card, you can also take advantage of credit cards that offer rewards for using them. Earning cash back or points toward travel is a great way to take advantage of getting something back each month. For instance, if you use a credit card that's giving away 50,000 airline points and you only use that card, so you can take advantage of this perk, and pay off the balance in full before getting charged any interest, that's considered a good way to utilize a credit card. Credit card companies use these offers to incentivize you to use the card but be careful because the card company will notice you using these offers and they'll occasionally increase your spending limit in the hopes that you'll overspend. That's why you should never use a credit card on purchases that you don't have the cash on hand to pay for.

Student loans are another great example of bad debt. While many articles circulating on the internet say student, loans are good debt because the return on investment comes in the form of knowledge, the reality is that once you graduate and start a career, your student loans turn into bad debt. Ideally, we would all like the loans we take out for an education to pay us back in the long run, but before they do, you need to pay them off entirely and for some people, that can take decades. So, while your current job is generating revenue for yourself, your loans are accruing interest while you struggle to pay the minimum each month. There's also no guarantee that you'll even get a specific return on your investment for student loan debt because there is no guarantee that you will get a career that pays well enough to afford those loans. This is why I question some of the things going on in our current education system with student loans being a cash cow for the government, colleges, and banks.

A mortgage on your home can be a good and bad form of debt depending on the circumstances. Many people think that a mortgage is good debt simply because it's something they plan to pay off and they feel they can sell their home for a profit in the future. Even if you plan to sell your house someday, the market must be right for you to make a profit. Luckily, home values typically do rise if you look at the prices in 7-year periods. So, buyers that plan on living in a home for at least 7 years will often see their home's value rise. A great benefit with mortgages is that they come with lower interest rates than that of credit cards and you can also tap into the equity that you build in a home over time with home equity lines of credit (HELOC) or home equity loans. These loans can be used to fund home improvements, pay for your child's education, pay down higher interest credit card debt, and even be used towards other investment opportunities that may generate a better rate of return than the interest rate for the HELOC or home equity loan. Owning a home also comes with some tax breaks like writing off property taxes and the amount of interest you pay on your mortgage each year. Debt that you can write off on your taxes should also be considered good debt.

Even if you've paid off your house and have no debt on it, it's still a liability. The is due to cash flow. The average person has a job where money comes in and they use it to pay for their house by giving it to the bank through a mortgage. A liability takes money from your pocket, while an asset puts money in your pocket. So, your house is not an asset because the cash flow is going out, to the bank through a mortgage, which makes it a liability. A house is not necessarily an asset when you live in it, even when it's paid off, because you still must pay for insurance and keep up with repairs and regular maintenance. Now let's say someone takes out a mortgage on a property not to live in full time, but to use as a rental property. The tenants pay the owner and that money is used to pay the mortgage, cover insurance, and keep up with repairs. That house is now an asset because it's putting money in your pocket and taking it out of someone else's. Not everyone can be in this situation where they can make their house an asset, because everyone has a different lifestyle and financial situation and there's nothing wrong with that. Regardless of your situation, it's important to know how something like a mortgage can be a good debt when used correctly.

Another way a mortgage can be a bad debt is if you buy a home without paying any regards to your Debt-To-Income (DTI) ratio. A DTI ratio is derived by dividing your monthly debt payments by your monthly gross income. This ratio is a percentage that lenders use to determine how well you manage monthly debts and if you can afford to repay a loan. The highest DTI ratio that a homebuyer can have for a mortgage is 43%. The lower your DTI, the better terms and lower interest rate you may receive for your mortgage. Personally, I think the equation used to determine your

DTI ratio is flawed because it's based off your gross income rather than your net income. Basing your DTI off your gross income rather than your net income can be misleading since a chunk of your gross income goes to taxes. This is misleading, and it can cause people to mess up their monthly budget because they end up overspending on a home thinking they can afford more just because of their DTI ratio. This is what leads nearly 40 million U.S. households to be "house poor", which means they own a home they can't easily afford[40]. In my opinion, I think you should always keep your DTI ratio below 36%, which includes a mortgage, credit card, and car loans.

Have you ever heard the saying "cash poor and house rich"? When someone is cash poor and house rich, they are living beyond their means with their home which prevents them from being able to afford regular living expenses each month because much of their income is going to housing. Their expensive mortgage and high property tax payments make it nearly impossible to cover other expenses, save for emergencies, or invest for the future. So, while they may have an enormous beautiful house, they're struggling to make ends meet each month.

A home will determine your lifestyle and dictate your budget along with your future income needs and expenses. That's why many older couples end up selling their homes to "downsize". It's not necessarily because they want a smaller house with less space, it's because they can't afford their house anymore with their current lifestyle, especially after retirement. To avoid becoming house poor, you need to determine what an appropriate house and lifestyle look like for you.

When you begin looking for your first home or are looking to upgrade to your next home, use this simple calculation. Think of the ideal home you would like to live in, with the right amount of rooms and the perfect location, then take the value of that home and divide it by 30% (.30). This will give you your minimum net annual income that you need to support your lifestyle in that house. Now multiply that income by 4% (.04) to see how much you would need saved up at retirement to continue your lifestyle in that home. For a

---

[40] State of the Nation's Housing 2017 Report, Joint Center for Housing Studies of Harvard University

1-million-dollar home you would need at least $300,000 ($1,000,000 x .30) of net annual income to support your lifestyle in that home and $7,500,000 ($300,000/.04) of invested money at retirement to maintain this lifestyle for the rest of your life. Trust me, you won't see a bank give you that information when you get pre-approved for a mortgage. If you feel like buying a home is the right choice for you, make sure you research property values, interest rates, and home appreciation averages for the area.

For some people, renting a place to live in is a better choice financially than taking out a mortgage for a home. If you're in a transitional period of your life or only planning to be in a specific area for less than 2 years, it may make more sense to find a place to rent rather than buy. The national average for rent in the United States is $1,400 a month. If we look at this scenario, that's an expense of $16,800 over the course of a year, $84,000 over 5 years, and $168,000 over 10 years. After 30 years, that's $504,000 and in that instance, would owning a home would be a better choice? Another thing to consider is if you would be better off owning a home and then renting it out once you move out to create another paycheck for yourself. This is why it's crucial to evaluate each situation when it comes to housing to determine if it's a better investment for you to buy or rent. When you rent, you'll never get that money back and the person who owns the property is gaining the benefit of using it as an asset at your expense.

Some financial gurus say that all debt is evil no matter what kind it is, and they advise you to never use debt at all. For a large majority of people, debt certainly is a bad idea because they don't know how to use it correctly and they can't control their spending. The reality though is that we live in a time where debt is very necessary especially when it comes to purchasing a home or a car. Sadly, for many people, it's also how we fund our education. The problem is that too many people take out loans and go into debt for the wrong things like a home appliance, a car modification, or even a vacation. You should never under any circumstance use debt to finance your fun at the expense of your future.

Even I have made poor decisions when it comes to debt. After I bought my current townhome, I went out and bought a Mercedes C63 AMG, a car that I thought would make me happy. The price of that car was $65,000, which I didn't have at the time, so what did I do? I went into debt to buy it. The thing is, I didn't even need that car because I had another vehicle that was completely paid off and had no issues, but I foolishly traded it in when I purchased my Mercedes and took out a loan for what was left after the trade in value. I ended up with a 4-year loan that cost me $1,000 a month. Over those 4 years, I would be flushing $48,000 down the drain because that car depreciated the moment I drove it off the lot and I could never earn money from it. If I had kept my other car, I could have had an extra $1,000 a month to invest in something that would make money for my future. This is where opportunity cost comes in.

Opportunity cost represents the benefits that you can potentially miss out on when choosing one alternative over another and it can easily by overlooked if you're not careful. Understanding the potential missed opportunities by making one choice over another allows for better decision-making. The formula for calculating an opportunity cost is simply the difference between the expected returns of each option. Say that you have Option A - buy the Mercedes with a monthly payment of $1,000 and Option B - invest the monthly payment of $1,000. Which has the potential for a better profit? I chose the wrong option and my opportunity cost for this purchase was the return that I gave up by not investing $1,000 each month. Had I invested $1,000 each month into the S&P 500 at an annual rate of return of 8% for a 4-year period, I would have turned that $48,000 into $56,350.

Good debt is used for one thing and one thing only – to generate more money. Good debt is typically defined as debt used to finance something that will increase in value in the future. The beauty of good debt is that it's essentially an investment because you're spending money now in the expectation of getting your money back, and perhaps some profit on top of that in the future. Because you're spreading the payments out over many months or years, you can buy the item you're financing immediately instead of having to wait and save up enough money to buy it all at once. On top of that, good debt tends to carry a relatively low interest rate in the single digits. When not used carefully, good debt can easily turn into bad debt. When it comes to good debt, think of those things that will give you a return and appreciate over time. The risks of good debt occur when we make assumptions about the future based on our hopes for the future and our typical results in the past. It's important to remember that there are no guarantees when taking on good debt.

When I purchased my McLaren, the car loan was still bad debt because I'm not getting any return from the car and it is not generating me any cash flow. The purchase itself some might even call stupid, but I wanted to use debt to purchase the vehicle in a way that would benefit me, so I made a strategic plan and followed through with it. Before I even seriously considered this large and potentially foolish purchase, I had to make sure that I had the two times price of the vehicle saved up between my cash accounts at the bank and my investment accounts. I chose to put 30% of the vehicle's price as my down payment and finance the remaining 70%. For the down payment, I used my credit card and immediately paid off the balance the next day. By doing so, I took advantage of the points that my card provides me such as airfare discounts and cash back. The remaining 70% was financed at an interest rate that is below what I average in my personal investment account. I now use my personal investment account to make the monthly payments and if I continue to generate a return above my interest payment on the loan, my payments will continue to come from the investment account without affecting my account balance.

You should now have a relatively good understanding of both the good and the bad ways to use debt. Wise borrowers try to maximize good debt and minimize bad debt. Credit card debt is especially dangerous because of the high interest rates and the late fees that can start piling up if you fall behind on your payments. There are no downsides to using a credit card to make purchases, if you can commit to paying off the card before interest accrues. When you fall into the habit of buying things you can't afford by putting them on plastic, you're digging yourself into a deep pit that will cost you a lot of money to escape from. It helps if you try to think like an investor every time you do something that will increase your debt. Ask yourself, *"Do I expect to make a profit off this purchase?"* If the answer is no, then consider waiting until you can pay cash to buy the item. Investing money is also important for your future but if you have high interest credit card debt it doesn't make sense to go out and invest your money to get a 6% ,8%, or even 15% return when you're paying over 20% interest towards your credit card debt. Pay off that debt as fast as possible first, and then go and invest your money and begin building your wealth.

Always remember that it is possible to overuse good debt, so you should always be cautious. The wealthy use debt to create a life, not finance one, and if you aren't using your debt to create a life, you should consider changing your mindset on debt and how you plan to use it. No matter how you plan to use loans to create a life for yourself, you should first get rid of toxic debt as soon as possible. If you're budgeting realistically, actively paying off your debt, and saving money, you're one big step closer to financial freedom. Once you're on the path to financial freedom, it's time to start thinking of investments.

Exercise 3:
Your Current Liabilities

Liabilities are a part of your overall financial health and it's important to keep them in check. Liabilities reveal a lot about your relationship with money and debt. For example, they can highlight your financial mistakes and restrict your ability to build up assets for your future. Having liabilities doesn't necessarily mean you're in bad financial shape though. To understand the effects of your liabilities, you'll need to put them in context.

It's important to take inventory of all your current liabilities. As you should have already determined your current net worth, you have a list of all your current liabilities and their outstanding balances. Let's go one step further to determine the types of liabilities that you have and look at your good debt versus your bad debt.

Next to each of your current liabilities I want you to write down the current interest rate and your current monthly payment.

Which of your liabilities have an interest rate below 5%?

Which of your liabilities have an interest rate above 5%?

Any of your current liabilities that have an interest rate above 5% are most likely a form of bad debt and you should research to see if there are any ways to lower the interest rate, allowing you to pay down that liability sooner.

For credit cards, can you transfer the balance to a lower rate card? For student loans, are you able to consolidate into loans with a lesser rate? For any auto loan on a vehicle you purchased, can you refinance into a lower rate? Research this potential for any of your current liabilities with an interest rate above 5%.

Liabilities can become problematic, especially if they significantly exceed your assets, leaving you with a negative net worth. This will hinder your ability to pursue financial goals, such as building your emergency fund or saving and investing for your retirement. No matter how much or what kind of debt you have, you must have a plan to pay each liability down. For bad debt, the sooner you can pay it off, the better. The more time you have to build up your assets for your future, the less weight your liabilities will carry.

"How many millionaires do you know who have become wealthy by investing in savings accounts? I rest my case."

Robert G. Allen

Chapter 8

Investing 101, Create Your Future Paycheck

Now that you've established the foundation for your financial plan (your current net worth), you know the cash flow on the first floor of your house (your net income and expenses), you can now focus on the second floor which is investing for your future. To create a future paycheck for yourself, you need to invest, but there are many different aspects to investing that can make it seem intimidating and feel overwhelming. Investing has its own language and the people who speak the language often talk right over our heads. While there are many ways to invest, most people don't know the first thing about how it works, which is why I'm going to explain the basics of investing and the different ways it can benefit you.

The great thing about investing is that you don't necessarily have to actively do it every day. Our time is precious, and investing can really benefit us if we do it in a way that we are able to grow our money while we sleep, spend time with family, and even work at our regular job. When we invest our money to create a passive income stream for our future, we enable ourselves to earn money without physically working for it. That's why investing is so important, especially for millennials because the sooner we start, the longer we have for our money to grow into a future paycheck. There is no time like the present to begin investing. That statement is half correct, there was a better time than the present and that was when you were 18. Back then, money was not as high of a priority as it may be today for you, so the second-best time to begin investing is right now!

Investing is non-negotiable if you want to grow your wealth, achieve your financial goals, and have enough money to retire comfortably one day when you no longer wish to work for a paycheck. Simply saving money in a bank account is not enough, so don't confuse saving with investing. Don't expect Social Security, if it even still exists, to be a large part of your retirement either because while the government says it will be around for us when we retire, nothing is guaranteed.

You should never rely too heavily on others when planning how to live your future. In today's world, the average retirement benefit from Social Security for a retiree is roughly $16,380 per year. Do you think you could live on less than $20,000 a year? Social Security trustees have also announced that the Social Security fund you have been paying taxes to year after year will be completely depleted by 2034. Personal Capital did a study in 2018 which found that 29% of Generation X and 15% of millennials are expecting Social Security to be their primary source of income when they retire[41]. If you expected the same, then I have bad news for you because it's just not feasible. We really need to start looking out for ourselves and our futures and the way to do that is to start investing money now, so we can build a paycheck for our future.

Age	Month	Week	Day
20	$216	$54	$6.97
30	$484	$121	$15.61
40	$1,140	$285	$36.77
50	$3,070	$767	$99.03

I created this chart to show how much money you would need to contribute daily, weekly, and monthly starting at the age of 20, 30, 40, and 50 to reach $1 million dollars by age 65. In each of these examples, I assume an annual rate of return of 8%. As you can see, the longer you wait to invest, the more money you would need to save later in life. If you're 20, you would need to save just $6.97 a day whereas if you do not start until you're 50, you would need to save $99.03 a day to reach $1 million dollars by the age of 65.

---

[41] Personal Capital, 2018

Timing is everything and we really can't afford to put investing off any longer.

The number one reason investing is so important is to outpace inflation. As I've mentioned before, investing itself is designed so that if you invest $1 today, you have more than $1 tomorrow. Inflation is the enemy; it's the cost of goods and services increasing as time goes on so think of it as the erosion of your money. Back in 2005, the average cost for a movie ticket was $6.41 but at the end of 2018 the average cost for a movie ticket was $9.14. This is because of inflation. The cost of everything rises over time whether it's a house, a car, college tuition, groceries, or a movie ticket, with some costs rising quicker than others. If you deposit $100 into your bank account and the bank pays you 1% interest, after one year you would have $101 in your bank account. If inflation is 2% over the course of the same year, a $100 product would cost $102 at the end of the year. Inflation in this example made you lose $1 of purchasing power.

Anytime your savings isn't growing at the same rate as inflation, you're losing money. The average annual rate of inflation in the US is 3%[42], but remember, that is just an average and some of your expenses may be growing at a much faster rate of inflation. Let's assume that you started working when you were 18 and every day you saved $5 into your bank account and the bank paid you 1% interest every year. If you continue to do this every day until you retire at the age of 65 you would have saved up $108,000. That really isn't a lot of money to retire with. Now let's assume that you do the same thing starting at 18, but instead of saving the $5 each day, you invest it at an annual rate of return of 8%. When you retire at the age of 65 you would have $932,000.

You simply cannot save your way to wealth nor can you save your way to building a future that pays you. Compound interest and time are your best friends and we as millennials have a lot of time for compound interest to work its magic. Inflation can hurt you well before retirement too, especially if you're saving money steadily for a goal like a college fund or a down payment on a house. If you're simply saving your money in the bank and not investing it, the

---

[42] Zacks.com, November 2018

purchasing power of that money can very well be declining as it sits in your savings.

Investing, in its simplest form, is what happens if you trade your money today for more money in the future. In this chapter, I'll cover employer provided plans, retirement accounts, the basics of investing, and the importance of the stock market including why it exists and why we should take advantage of it. The first thing to understand is that contrary to popular belief, you do not need a large amount of money to start investing, in fact some investment platforms require no minimum at all. All too often I hear people say they can't start investing because they don't have enough money, and that's just not true.

The amount of money you can start investing with of course varies depending on your own personal situation. If you're young and don't have many expenses, you can be more aggressive with your savings and investing and should consider investing at least 30% of your net income. If you're older and have more liabilities, you should aim to invest a minimum of 15% of your net income. The best way to do this is by automating your investment contributions. You want your money invested before you even see it, so that it's out of sight, out of mind, and you're not tempted to spend it. This money will benefit you more if you let it grow for your future. Just keep in mind that the longer you wait, the more you lose out on compounding interest.

I get a lot of questions about investing and retirement planning from millennials such as *"how and where should I save for retirement?"* and *"should I participate in my companies 401(k)?"* Most millennials don't even know what an IRA and Roth IRA are or how investing works. In this chapter, I'm going to answer all those questions and more, so let's start breaking it down.

A 401(k) is the most common type of employer provided retirement plan. If your employer offers a 401(k) or similar retirement savings plan, it's important that you take advantage of it. With a 401(k) you make pre-tax or post-tax contributions from your salary or wages. Pre-tax contributions will help to lower your overall taxable income for the year. Let's assume that you earn $100,000 for the year and contribute $5,000 into your employer's 401(k). The $5,000 contribution would be deducted from your taxable income, so you would only pay income tax on $95,000 that year. For post-tax contributions, you pay income tax on the contributions in the year you contribute to the 401(k) and there is no deduction from your taxes. A 403(b) is a similar retirement account that works the same but is only available to employees of nonprofits or government agencies.

One of the most important reasons to take advantage of a 401(k) is if your employer provides a contribution match, because it's literally free money. Assume that your employer offers a 100% match on all your contributions each year, up to a maximum of 3% of your annual income. If you earn $100,000, the maximum amount your employer contributes each year is $3,000. To maximize this benefit, you must also contribute $5,000. If you contribute more than 3% of your salary, the additional contributions are unmatched.

A partial matching setup with an upper limit is most common. Assume that your employer matches 50% of your contributions that equal 6% of your salary. If you earn $100,000, the contributions equal to 6% of your salary, or $6,000, are eligible for matching. However, your employer only matches 50%, meaning the total matching benefit is still capped at $3,000. Under this matching setup, you must contribute twice as much to your retirement to reap the full benefits of your employer matching.

Many 401(k) plans only allow you to invest into mutual funds, which are professionally managed investment funds that pool money from multiple investors to purchase securities, or investments traded on a secondary market. Stocks and bonds are the most common types of securities. A stock is a type of security that signifies ownership in a company so when you own stock in a company, you own a small piece of that company. A bond is a debt security and represents a loan made by an investor (you) to a company or the government, sort of like an I.O.U.

Here's a simple way to understand the difference between a mutual fund, a stock, and a bond. Imagine being in a bakery filled with a wide variety of cookies. Each cookie represents a different stock or bond. You find one cookie that you like, and you purchase it. There's nothing wrong with buying just one cookie, but there are a few risks associated with it. What if your cookie goes stale? What if you drop your cookie and it gets dirty? What happens after you eat your cookie? Your investment in the cookie is gone. The same can hold true by purchasing a single stock or bond. You are risking your money on a single company. So instead of buying just one cookie at the bakery, imagine buying a jar of cookies. Inside the jar are multiple cookies, so if one were to go stale or get dropped, there are still plenty of cookies left. The same goes for a mutual fund, which is nothing more than the cookie jar holding many stocks, bonds, cash, and other investments to create diversification. Have you ever heard the saying *"don't put all your eggs in one basket"*? It's the same concept because if one of your investments doesn't do well, you have others to rely on.

When you do pre-tax contributions into a 401(k), both the contributions and the earnings grow tax deferred. This means that you do not pay any income tax on your contributions or earnings until you begin to withdraw them. When you being to withdraw them, you will pay income tax on the money as if it were income you earned in the year you made the withdrawal. There are some rules that you must follow when participating in a 401(k). You cannot withdraw from a 401(k) until you are over the age of 59 ½. If you do, you will not only pay income tax on the withdrawal, but you will also pay 10% of the withdrawal as a penalty to the government. There are a few exceptions to this rule. You may withdraw funds from your 401(k) before turning 59 ½ penalty free if you are using the withdrawals for tuition or other college expenses, using the funds for a first-time home purchase, have a medical expense that is more than 10% of your gross annual income, or if you are required by a court to provide funds to a divorced spouse, a child, or other dependents. Even though the 10% penalty is waived in these instances, you would still be required to pay income tax on the withdrawal.

Another benefit of taking advantage of a 401(k) is that the contributions are made directly from your paycheck every pay period. This allows for dollar-cost averaging into your investments. Dollar-cost averaging means you're investing a fixed amount of money into the same securities at regular intervals over a long period of time. The number of shares in each security purchased every pay period will vary depending on the share price of the investment at the time of the purchase. When the share value rises, your money will buy fewer shares per dollar invested. When the share price is down, your money will get you more shares. Dollar-cost averaging can be done in any type of investment account and this strategy is particularly attractive for new investors just starting out because it's a way to slowly but surely build wealth, especially if you're starting out with a smaller amount.

Something else to understand with a 401(k) is that you're limited with how much you can contribute. The contribution limits change annually, so it's always wise to research those limits at the beginning of each year. Depending on your own financial situation, it may be beneficial to contribute up to the maximum limit into your employer's 401(k). This is not a one size fits all approach and it's important that you educate yourself about your employer's specific plan and eligible investments. This book will not help you determine how much you should contribute to your 401(k) or any investment account for that matter, but it will give you a broad understanding of how these types of plans, accounts, and investments work. It is always wise to consult with a financial advisor when you are unsure about investing or where to begin.

An individual retirement account (IRA), is another tax-deferred investment account that allows you to invest money for retirement. When you contribute to an IRA, your contributions can be deducted from your income for the year much like a 401(k). If you earn $100,000 for the year and contribute $2,500 into your IRA, the $2,500 contribution would be deducted from your taxable income, and you would only pay tax on $97,500 for the year. An IRA has a lower contribution limit than a 401(k) and the contribution limits may change annually. Like a 401(k), you cannot withdraw from an IRA until you are over the age of 59 ½ or you'll have to pay income tax on the withdrawal along with a 10% penalty to the government. The same exceptions to this rule apply, allowing you to withdraw penalty free if you are using the withdrawals for tuition, a first-time home purchase, medical expenses over 10% of your gross annual income, or court ordered payments. While the 10% penalty is waived like in the 401(k), you'll still be required to pay income tax on the withdrawal.
Along with the traditional IRA, there are several types of other IRA accounts including the Roth IRA, SEP IRA, and SIMPLE IRA. It's important for millennials to understand each of these types of IRA accounts, as taking advantage of them could be very beneficial.

In a Roth IRA, contributions aren't tax-deductible, but the money that you contribute grows tax-free and distributions are tax-free once you're over the age of 59 ½. This means that when you retire, you can withdraw from your Roth IRA account without paying any income tax on your withdrawals. Here's an example of how you could potentially build a million-dollar Roth IRA. Let's look at a married couple, each of them 30 years old and each earning $50,000 annually for a total gross income of $100,000 and a net income of $78,000 after taxes. If the couple were to contribute $500 each month, or roughly 7.7% of their total net income, and were able to average an 8% annual rate of return, at the age of 65 the couple would have $1,146,941. Every single penny of that million dollars would be tax free for their use in retirement. This is especially important for millennials to consider because time is on our side and it's a great opportunity to create a nice amount of tax-free income for our future.

Roth IRA contribution limits are the same as a traditional IRA and are subject to change on an annual basis. The catch is that not everyone can contribute to a Roth IRA. There are limitations based on your total gross annual income which varies depending on your marital status. Once your income is over the limit you're restricted from contributing to a Roth IRA. These income limits are also subject to change annually, so it's wise to research the contribution and income limits at the beginning of each year to ensure that you do not go over them, otherwise you may face a penalty from the government.

Many millennials are self-employed, whether we're creating our own businesses, working as independent contractors, or working as freelancers. A report from the Center for Retirement Research at Boston College highlights that fewer than 40% of millennials are participating in employer provided plans such as a 401(k). This is because many of us have our own businesses that don't have a retirement plan in place and some of us do freelance work and don't work enough hours to qualify for a company's retirement plan.

A Simplified Employee Pension (SEP) IRA is a retirement account specially designed for those who are self-employed and receiving 1099 income. If you are a worker earning a salary or wage, your employer reports your annual earnings at the end of each year on a Form W-2. If you're an independent contractor or self-employed, you receive a Form 1099. Contributions into a SEP IRA are tax deductible just like a traditional IRA, however contribution limits are much higher than the traditional IRA or Roth IRA. There are no income limitations for the SEP IRA. Rules for withdrawal and taxation on withdrawals from a SEP IRA are the same as a traditional IRA. Generally, SEP IRAs are best for self-employed people or small-business owners with few or no employees.

The Savings Incentive Match Plan for Employees (SIMPLE) IRA is also intended for small businesses and self-employed individuals. It too follows the same taxation rules for withdrawals as a traditional IRA, but unlike SEP IRAs, SIMPLE IRAs allow employees to make contributions to their accounts, and the employer is required to make contributions as well. All contributions into a SIMPLE IRA are tax-deductible. The SIMPLE IRA employee contribution limits are subject to change on an annual basis.

Investments held in IRAs can include a wide range of financial products such as stocks, bonds, mutual funds, ETFs, cash, and even real estate. The accounts we have been discussing so far are all considered qualified investment accounts. Qualified investment accounts receive certain tax advantages when money is deposited into the account. The contributions into a qualified investment account can be deducted from your taxable income in the year they are made and earnings on the investments can be delayed as taxable income until they are withdrawn. This is not the only way that you can invest for the future. There are also non-qualified investment accounts to consider.

Non-qualified investment accounts do not receive preferential tax treatment. This means that they do not allow for any contributions to be deductible from your taxes and earnings are not deferred until you begin making withdrawals or when you sell an investment. In a non-qualified investment account, you can invest as little or as much as you'd like in a year and can withdraw from the account at any time. Money that you invest into a non-qualified account is money that you've already received through income sources and paid income tax on, so when you sell an investment, you only pay tax on the realized gains, which is any money above what you had contributed. Money that you contribute into a non-qualified account is considered your cost basis or principal. When you withdraw your cost basis, you are not taxed again as you have already paid income tax on it.

Any value in your account that is above your cost basis represents growth and would be subject to capital gains tax. For example, if you invest $1,000 into a non-qualified investment account and in a year's, time earn an 8% rate of return, you have earned $80 on your investment. Your balance in your non-qualified investment account is now $1,080. When you sell the investment, you would have to pay capital gains tax on $80. How long you hold an investment inside of your non-qualified investment account will determine what type of capital gains tax you pay.

There are two types of capital gains tax, short-term capital gains tax and long-term capital gains tax. Short-term capital gains tax is a tax on profits from the sale of an investment held for one year or less. Short-term capital gains tax rates equal your ordinary income tax rate, very similar to a qualified account withdrawal. Long-term capital gains tax is a tax on profits from the sale of an investment held for more than a year. Long-term capital gains tax rates are 0%, 15%, or 20% depending on your taxable income for the year and your filing status. Long-term capital gains tax rates are generally lower than short-term capital gains tax rates.

So, should you invest into non-qualified or qualified investment accounts? That's a great question to ask your financial advisor. In most cases, I suggest you build a balance of both non-qualified and qualified investment accounts for your future. This will provide you with many more options and greater flexibility.

Let's look at an individual that's ready to retire today. They never worked with a financial advisor and only ever contributed to their 401(k), contributing the maximum amount they could each year. Upon retirement, this individual has $2,000,000 in their 401(k). All this money is qualified and subject to income tax when withdrawals are made. If this person needs $50,000 a year to support their current lifestyle they would need to withdrawal substantially more than $50,000, as they would need to pay taxes on every dollar earned. Had the individual also been saving and investing in a non-qualified investment account during their working years, they could have had the flexibility of withdrawing funds without having as large of an impact on their taxable income each year. If this person would have further taken advantage of a Roth IRA, they would have the flexibility of withdrawing funds tax free.

Have you ever heard someone say that investing in the stock market is just like gambling at a casino? While investing and gambling both involve risk and choice, specifically the risk of capital (money) with the hopes of future profit, gambling is typically a short-lived activity while investing can last a lifetime. Investing in the stock market typically carries with it a positive expected return on average over the long run. Investing is the process of allocating funds or committing capital (money) to an investment like stocks, with the expectation of generating an income or profit. The expectation of a return comes in the form of income or an increase in the value of the investment. With gambling, the house always has a mathematical advantage over each player and that advantage increases the longer they continue to play, while the stock market constantly appreciates in value over the long term. This doesn't mean that a gambler will never hit the jackpot, and it also doesn't mean that investing in the stock market will always produce a positive return. It simply means that over time, if you continue investing, the odds will be in your favor as an investor but not so much as a gambler.

People that truly think investing in the stock market is the same as gambling don't understand how it really works. It's true that some people treat investing like gambling because they haven't taken the time to learn how to invest properly. Some only search for a "hot" stock tip and hope it wins big, like spinning the roulette wheel in a casino. One thing that gambling and investing do have in common is the importance of keeping your emotions in check.

Let's look at some of the most common forms of investing and how they operate. As I mentioned earlier, purchasing a stock means you're purchasing a small percentage of ownership in a company. Companies issue and sell stock to raise funds to operate their businesses. When a company first offers their stock to outside investors it's called an Initial Public Offering (IPO) and when you purchase stock, you become a shareholder, as you have bought a piece of the corporation and have a claim to a part of its assets and earnings. It is important to note that the value of a share of stock is 100% determined by what someone is willing to pay for it.

When you are a shareholder of a company, you are entitled to a few perks. One major perk is that you could influence a company's decisions through voting. If you own 51% or more of a company, you can pretty much influence the company to do whatever you want. If you own a smaller share you would need to partner up with other shareholders to influence important decisions within the company.

Some companies pay dividends to their shareholders. Dividends are payments to investors based on the companies' earnings and can be paid as cash or in the form of additional shares of stock. Startups and some high-growth companies such as those in the technology sector usually don't pay dividends because all the company's profits are being reinvested back into the company, so they can maintain a higher than average rate of growth. Investors, particularly retired investors, like the steady stream of income that dividend stocks provide and like the ability to reinvest the dividends to buy more shares of stock. Larger more established companies with more predictable profits are often the best dividend payers. Companies in certain sectors such as oil and gas, financials, healthcare and pharmaceuticals, historically have produced the largest dividends.

While there's the ability to earn good money with dividend producing stocks, most of the money you hear about being made in the stock market is capital gains through the selling shares of a stock at a higher price than when you had initially bought it for. It's reasonable to assume that as a company grows larger and becomes more profitable, people will be willing to pay more for the company, and vice versa. Remember, you only gain or lose money on a stock when you sell it. If the stock price goes down, you technically didn't lose any money and if the price goes up you technically didn't make any money. You only realize a gain or loss when you sell the stock. When you invest for your future it's for long-term growth and you should not pay much attention to the day to day fluctuations in the stock's price.

How often do you purchase something for yourself from a publicly traded company? If you can't start your day without stopping at Starbucks, consider this – in 1992, Starbucks listed their stock in an IPO. If you would have invested $6 daily into their stock instead of spending it on their coffee, you would now have over $1.5 million dollars of stock. That sounds better than the $40,000 you spent on their coffee since 1992 now doesn't it? When it comes to investing in publicly traded companies, consider the companies you know and love not just as a place to purchase from, but also as a company you would potentially want to own a piece of.

Just like us, many times a company may feel it's necessary to take on debt to achieve their goals in the form of issuing bonds. Most bonds are created for the expansion of a company. A bond is a fixed income investment that represents a loan made by an investor (you) to a borrower. A bond is referred to as a fixed income instrument since bonds traditionally pay a fixed interest rate (coupon) to their debtholders (investors). Think of a bond as a sort of loan between you and a corporation or the government, and in this instance, you're the bank. The government commonly issues bonds to borrow money to fund roads, schools, or other infrastructure. Corporations will often issue bonds to grow their business, buy property and equipment, undertake profitable projects, for research and development, or to hire employees. Bond prices are inversely correlated with interest rates, which means they react in an opposite manner. When interest rates go up, bond prices fall and vice-versa.

As with any debt, there is an interest rate associated with bonds. The higher the risk of the company not repaying the debt, the higher the yield of their bonds. A bond's yield is the return an investor realizes on a bond. The bond's yield is paid to the bondholder (investor) for a predetermined frequency and period of time. The length of time that a bond exists, otherwise known as its term, directly affects how much money a bondholder can make if they hold the bond until it matures. Maturity is a fancy word for saying when the bond pays back the initial investment (principal). Just like with stocks, a bond's price can fluctuate based on its perceived value. If people think a company will default on its debt, the price of the bond can go down. On the flip side, if people think that it's highly unlikely that a company will default on its debt, the price goes up. Regardless of price, the amount paid per bond will remain the same, so the cheaper a bond is the higher it's yield will be. Since bonds better retain their income and are less risky than stocks, people add bonds into their portfolio, as a way, to lower overall risk.

An exchange-traded fund (ETF) gets its name since it's traded on a stock exchange just like a stock. A stock exchange is a collection of markets where buying, selling, and issuing shares of publicly-held companies takes place, such as the New York Stock Exchange (NYSE). A stock exchange and stock market are interchangeable terms. The stock market opens for trading at 9:30am EST closes at 4:00pm EST Monday through Friday, except for holidays. Mutual funds do not trade on a stock exchange and can only be bought or sold once the market has closed for the day, making them less liquid than a stock or ETF. Taxes are a significant expense in life, so it's nice to avoid paying them when we can, legally. If you're looking to avoid taxes, specifically capital gains taxes, ETFs have a big advantage over mutual funds. When you invest in an ETF, you only incur capital gains taxes when you sell the fund. Mutual fund investors will pay capital gains taxes whenever the shares within the fund are traded by the managers of the fund.

A lifecycle fund is common in most retirement accounts such as a 401(k) or 403(b). The goal of a lifecycle fund is to be a one stop shop when it comes to retirement investing. Usually a lifecycle fund will have a name such as "Target Retirement 2040 Fund". These types of investments start out heavily invested in stocks and slowly over time transition into bonds. The year 2040, in this example, refers to the planned retirement date that an investor in the fund should have.

A common investment theme lately has been to focus on using index mutual funds or ETFs. Incredibly, half of all U.S. stock fund assets are now invested into index funds[43]. News reports, financial forums, and even Google queries, will often feature someone saying that the best way to invest is using index funds. At times many assume that index funds are a safer way to invest than the traditional routes such as stocks or bonds. An index fund is basically a fund that you could put your money into that will mimic the returns of stock market indexes, such as the S&P 500. If you invest into an S&P 500 index fund, your investment is going to do exactly what the S&P 500 does. So, when you invest into an index fund, you're investing in the entire market. If the S&P 500 moves up 5%, then you're going to make 5% on your investment. Likewise, if the S&P 500 moves down 10%, you're going to lose 10% on your investment.

---

[43] 2019 Morningstar Report

When you're investing in a fund, whether it be an index fund, a mutual fund, an ETF, or something else, someone is managing the fund and obviously must get paid. For many of these types of funds the fee is called an expense ratio. This fee is basically just a small percentage of the assets in the fund. Index funds, mutual funds, and ETFs all carry fees. One of the biggest reasons people like index funds so much is because of the "low fees". When you're investing in an index fund the fees tend to be lower because the people managing the index funds are simply tracking what the overall market does. This is called passive investing because the managers are not actively trying to beat the market.

The opposite of passive investing is active investing, which is when you're actively trying to beat the market index. If you invest in a fund that is actively investing, the managers are doing a lot more work, so they're going to charge you more fees. The idea is that the people who invest in the passive funds such as index funds, simply want to mimic what the market is doing. They don't want to pay someone to try and pick stocks or bonds, in an attempt, to outperform the market. If you're thinking *"why wouldn't I want someone to do a good job picking stocks and making me more money?"*, it's because it's very difficult. Most of the active funds that you could invest in don't even outperform the general market[44]. In a lot of investors' heads, it makes sense to invest in a passive fund, like an index fund, instead of investing in something active where the manager doesn't necessarily do a good job because at that point, what are you paying for? Index funds do provide diversification across their index as they allow you to have a small stake in every stock or bond that is part of the index. So far this may seem like a pretty good reason to use index funds over anything else, but there is flip side to this coin.

Diversification does not mean you that you don't have the ability to lose money. Think of the period of time from 2008-2009 during the Great Recession, where the entire market dropped more than 50%. It didn't matter if you were diversified between a bunch of stocks in an index, because they all got crushed.

This is a big thing that many investors forget. Even if you're invested in an index fund, you are still going to have to face

---

[44] S&P Dow Jones Indices, SPIVA U.S. Year End Report, 2017

potentially large drops. The market goes through cycles, it goes up and then it goes down, and eventually you will face the potential for losses even in an index fund. When that time comes, the only thing that's going to help you in that situation is if you have a solid plan and investment strategy that you stick to no matter what. So, when your emotions start running wild as the market drops, you're not going to do something stupid like so many people did in 2008. Prior to 2008 as the stock market was surging upwards, many investors were buying into index funds because of their return, which was the same as the stock market. They bought into these index funds without regard to the overall state of the economy. What many did not realize is that they were buying into these index funds at the peak of the market, and when the economy slowed down, and the market subsequently dropped, many people started to sell their index funds and other investments in a panic at a price below what they originally purchased them for. This resulted in many people losing large amounts of money. The moral of the story is that while index funds allow an inexpensive way to access an overall market index, you can't just blindly invest in them. In the decade following the Great Recession, many investors have again blindly invested into index funds because of the great return they've provided since the bottom of the market in 2009. One thing that many investors seem to have forgotten is that what goes up must come down and the same scenario can happen again.

The stock market will ebb and flow, with prices moving up and down every second while the market is open for trading, all due to fluctuations in supply and demand. If more people want to buy a specific investment, its market price will increase, and if more people want to sell a specific investment, its price will fall. This relationship between supply and demand is often tied to news reports issued at any given moment on an investment. Negative news will likely cause individuals to sell an investment, while positive news will likely cause individuals to buy an investment.

The terms used to describe the ups and downs when it comes to investing are a bear market and a bull market. A bear market is when you see the stock market in a contraction and moving downward. A bull market is when you see the stock market in an expansion and moving upward. There's pessimism during a bear market and optimism during a bull market. These metaphors are used because of how a bear and bull attack. A bear stands up on its hind legs before attacking downward on its prey. In keeping with the metaphor, a bear market starts at a high point and moves downward. A bull lowers its horns before attacking in an upward motion, and a bull market starts at a low point and then moves upward.

We have been in a bull market since March 2009, making it the longest bull market in history. This bull market came out of the Great Recession, when a bear market took over and the stock market dropped nearly 50% over a few months. Bull markets are followed by bear markets, and vice versa, with both often signaling the start of larger economic patterns. In other words, a bull market typically means investors are confident, which indicates economic growth, while a bear market shows investors are pulling back, indicating the economy may do the same. The good news is that the average bull market tends to far outlast the average bear market, which is why over the long term, you may have more consistent growth of your money by investing in stocks. The S&P 500, which is a stock market index that tracks the stocks of 500 large-cap U.S. companies, has historically returned an average of 8% annually. Based on that average, if you had invested $1,000 into the S&P 500 30 years ago, you would have around $10,000 today despite the numerous bear markets we've experienced in that time frame.

One of the most important decisions to make when you decide to invest is your asset allocation, or how you choose to distribute your investments. How are you going to split your money into different types of investments such as stocks or bonds? In asset allocation, stocks are considered a riskier investment than bonds. This risk is typically rewarded with higher returns. Generally, the younger you are, the higher your risk tolerance should be because your money has many years to ride out the ups and downs of investing. A 30-year-old's portfolio will look very different from that of an 80-year-old. Some experts suggest you follow the rule of 100, where you subtract your age from 100 and whatever the number is, that's how much of your portfolio should be invested in stocks with the rest in bonds. The rule of 100 is just a guideline and I highly suggest that you work with a financial advisor to determine your specific level of risk and asset allocation. This is such an important aspect of your future and it's not a one size fits all solution. While I agree with asset allocation, I have always felt that the breakdown of how to allocate assets is inaccurate.

Many experts say that at the age of 20, you should invest 80% of your money into stocks and 20% into bonds, while if you're 90 years old you should invest 10% of your money into stocks and 90% into bonds. If you follow just this guideline, you may be doing yourself a great disservice. While bonds are usually considered to be a safer investment than stocks, that's not always the case. There is not enough discussion about the many different types of bonds that exist and how, at certain points in time, they can carry just as much risk as stocks. Remember when I discussed interest rates and the Federal Reserve in Chapter 1 and I mentioned how over the past few years interest rates were on the rise? Well, if you were invested in bonds over the past few years as interest rates were going up, it's quite possible that depending on the types of bonds that you hold, they lost value. When interest rates go up, bond prices go down, and vice-versa. Think of it like a seesaw.

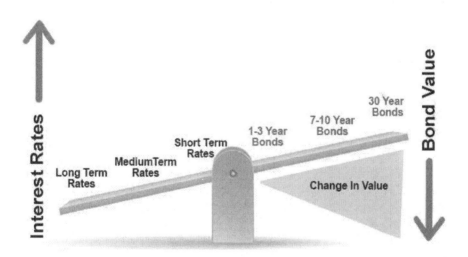

As you can see, on one end of the seesaw you have the interest rate of the bond and on the other end you have the value of the bond. The further you are from the center of the seesaw, the longer it takes for the bond to mature. This is the length of time until the bond is paid back by the corporation or government using your money. A bond with a shorter time till maturity will be closer to the center of the seesaw and move less in value as interest rates change. A bond with a longer maturity will be closer to the outer edge of the seesaw and will move more in value with the change in interest rates. Over the past few years as interest rates began to rise, the longer the duration of your bonds, the greater their value has been affected. This is a good example of why you cannot base your investment decisions on generalized templates. Doing so could cause you to invest in the wrong investments at certain times and negatively affect your account values. Again, you should seek the guidance of a financial advisor to help understand your personal needs, level of risk, and help assist you in finding the right investments that match your goals and needs.

While automating your contributions into investments is encouraged, you should never set and forget your investments. Markets rise and fall and so do investments. If you do not monitor your investments, you could be shorting yourself in the long run. If you don't want the risk or responsibility, it would be wise to work with someone, such as a financial advisor, who can monitor your investments for you. I believe that you should revisit your investments on a routine basis to see how they're performing and to determine if any adjustments are needed.

The next important part of investing is diversification. When you have a diversified portfolio, you're attempting to reduce your risk, but diversification can also reduce your potential profit and return. Let's assume that you have $30,000 and you invest it evenly across 3 different investments of $10,000 each. After one year, investment A went up 2%, investment B went down 3%, and investment C went up 10%. That means your $10,000 investment A turned into $10,200, your $10,000 investment B turned into $9,700, and your $10,000 investment C turned into $11,000. Overall your $30,000 investment grew to $30,900. If you would have invested all your $30,000 into investment C you would have experienced a much higher rate of return than if you invested all your $30,000 into investment B. Still, there is no guarantee that investment C would have produced such a large return. This is why you should always consider diversifying your money in more than a single investment. Good diversification is not just across stocks and bonds but also pertains to owning real estate and other types of investments. Remember, you can't avoid a bear market as an investor, but you can avoid the risk that comes from an undiversified portfolio.

Ever hear the saying *"buy low and sell high"*? This is the golden rule when it comes to investing, but far too often people do the opposite and purchase an investment when it's overvalued, only to turn around and sell the investment when it's undervalued. While it sounds so simple to avoid, when emotions are involved, the fear of missing out (FOMO) sets in and many chase a poor investment without first doing the proper research. Warren Buffett once said, *"it is wise to be fearful when others are greedy and greedy when others are fearful"*. If Walmart had a sale with 50% off all products, do you think people would avoid the store or flood the store to buy everything in sight? On the other hand, if Walmart raised their prices for all products by 50%, would people continue to shop there? All too often in the stock market, when the market has been growing, people tend to invest more into it, but when the market is coming down people tend to run in fear and pull their money out rather than investing more into it.

Let's switch gears for a moment and touch base on real estate investing. There is no one size fits all investment solution for everyone. For some, they may only invest in the stock market and may be quite successful, while others may only invest in real estate and be successful. Financial gurus tend to tout their respective field, whether it's the stock market or real estate, as the only way for you to invest for your future. That simply isn't the case and many times these recommendations are self-serving for these financial gurus. If there's only one thing you take from this chapter, let it be this - any investment such as stocks, bonds, mutual funds, ETFs, real estate, and even cash, could lose money if you don't understand what you're doing or the respective market that you're investing in.

Real estate went through a large mania and subsequent bubble in the mid-2000s. During that time, many people were buying multiple properties in the hopes of flipping them for a profit. This was brought on by a terribly mismanaged banking system that was giving money to virtually anyone that met two criteria: being a human and having a pulse. This mania caused home prices to skyrocket across the county and pushed many property values above what they were worth. When the housing bubble finally burst, many people lost a great deal of money. Those who took on too much debt to purchase properties could no longer afford them and were forced to sell the properties for pennies on the dollar. Everyone that participated in this bubble believed that home prices would only continue to rise. They did little research to the validity of the market and blindly took on debt to chase a buck. The moral of this story is that there's no such thing as a safe investment, otherwise we'd all be doing it. There's also no right or wrong way to go about investing. Any investment has the potential to earn you money as well as lose you money if you don't understand the investment or its market.

In today's world there are many real estate gurus who say that real estate is the best thing since sliced bread and there's nothing else that you should invest in. They say that real estate is the best investment because it's tangible and you can touch the property, unlike the stock market where you're only seeing a paper return. Many gurus have also said that real estate is never going away. I agree that real estate is never going away, but neither is the stock market. Companies will always need funding to grow their businesses and expand, therefore they will always need to issue stocks or bonds. One thing that people fail to realize is that many of today's largest real estate gurus were buying properties for pennies on the dollar during the housing bubble, which is how they built their empires. In the decade since the bubble, these properties have gained value simply by returning to their fair market value. I'm not trying to discredit these gurus, I'm simply highlighting the opportunity that they took advantage of during the housing bubble to purchase an investment when it was low in value.

The same can be said if you invested into the stock market during the same period of time. The average annual return for the S&P 500 from the bottom of 2009 until now has been 17.8%[45]. My warning to you is to understand the market today before you start investing whether it's in real estate, the stock market, or anything else. One investment is not better than the other as each carry their own unique ways to generate a profit, but each also carry their own unique levels of risk.

Inside of your investment accounts, you can invest in real estate in a different manner than simply buying a property. This

---

[45] Michael Batnick, The Irrelevant Investor, March 2019

investment is called a Real Estate Investment Trust (REIT). A REIT is a way for a group of investors to pool their money together to invest in real estate that they otherwise could not afford to buy outright on their own. Most REITs specialize in a specific sector and focus on a specific segment of real estate, whether it's cell towers, pipelines, office buildings, hotels, warehouses, land, or storage containers. REITs make their money on the leased space or property by collecting rents and then distributing the rental income as dividends to their shareholders.

So, is it better for you to invest in the stock market or in real estate? Both have their own advantages and disadvantages and you will want to know both sides of the coin, so you can make the best decision for yourself. A big advantage with stock market investing is that it's extremely easy to get started. If you wanted to invest in the stock market, you could open a brokerage account and start today. If you wanted to buy real estate, you would have to first find a property that you want to invest in and then you must secure financing for it, whether that be from other investors, your own cash, or by taking on debt. You must also source all the needed parties such as a real estate agent, contractor, and property manager. Real estate investing requires a lot of upfront work with buying the property, getting the property ready to rent, and hiring a property manager to do the day to day tasks. Therefore, real estate investing is much harder to get started with. I personally don't consider flipping real estate investing, because once you stop working, you stop getting paid.

Another advantage to stock market investing is that it's liquid. This means that you can convert your investments to cash in a short amount of time. Real estate is less liquid as it could take weeks or months for you to list your property for sale and then sell the property, getting your cash out of it. With stock market investing, there's no physical work required. If you purchase shares of a publicly traded company, you become a small owner of the company and can share in the profits without doing any of the work. With real estate investing there's more work required as you must ensure that all the bills are paid, ensure all the maintenance is done, and you have to make sure that your tenant pays on time. This is one of the reasons you could consider hiring a property manager. This way the property manager handles all the work. However, even if you have a property manager you still need to oversee them to make sure that they're doing their job.

An advantage with real estate investing is cash flow. With real estate investing you are creating a passive income stream because you'll be paid month after month from your tenants paying rent, even if you don't go to work. You could use this passive income stream to either reinvest into other investments or you can spend it. The stock market has forms of passive income such as dividend paying stocks, however dividend paying stocks usually pay less income that you get with real estate, depending on how much you have invested into the stock.

Another advantage to real estate investing is that it's tangible. When you own real estate, you can see it, touch it, and control and manage the property any way you want. This is one disadvantage to investing in the stock market, because it's a paper investment. What this means is that when you invest in a stock, you become one of the owners of a company on paper. If the managers of the company run it into the ground or it goes bankrupt, you can't get back your investment. This is one of the reasons diversification is important.

There are many questions that you need to ask yourself and educate yourself on before you decide which way to invest is best for you. You may even find that both could make sense for you. Either way, I recommend seeking a professional in the respective investment field that you wish to enter. Meet with them to learn about that investment's market, pros and cons, and any potential risks. As always, if any professional ever directs you to only consider that single investment field, run away. They clearly aren't looking out for your best interests. You want to be sure that you work with someone that will be unbiased and will only inform you to the ins and outs of their respective field.

Another important factor to consider with investing is your time horizon. Your time horizon is how long you plan to leave your money invested to grow until you need to use it. The longer your time horizon, the riskier your investments can be which is why younger investors are often encouraged to be more heavily weighted towards stocks than bonds. A longer time horizon would be greater than 10 years until you plan to use your investment, like investing for retirement when you're in your 30s. A medium time horizon is usually between 5 – 10 years until you plan to use your investments, like saving money for your children's college tuition. A short time horizon is usually less than 5 years until you plan to use your investments, like saving for a down payment on a house or a new vehicle. The shorter the time horizon, the less risk you want in your investments and the greater amount of liquidity you want available. The longer the time horizon, the more risk you can take with your investments and the less liquidity is a concern. An example of a less liquid investment could be real estate as it typically cannot be converted to cash in a short amount of time.

Investing involves risks, so you will need to determine your risk level by calculating the desired level of risk that you feel most comfortable with. Investing involves emotions, especially in periods of high fluctuations. At times investing can see quick and abrupt swings in the underlying investment's value, causing the media and public perception to swing from mania to panic in seconds and vice-versa. We've all heard about the Great Depression, the dot com bubble of the late 1990's, and the Great Recession of 2008 - 2009.

These can be very scary and overwhelming times and emotions can play a big role, so as an investor, you would want to educate yourself on the historical worst-case returns in any one year an asset class that you would consider investing in. An asset class is a grouping of comparable financial securities such as stocks, bonds, real estate, cash equivalents, etc. This will give you an idea of how much money you would feel comfortable losing if your investment has a bad year or series of bad years. Other factors affecting risk tolerance include your time horizon, your future earning capacity, your current and future obligations, and the presence of other assets such as a home or an inheritance. In general, you can take on a greater amount of risk with your investable assets when you have a longer time horizon and other more stable funds available for the near future. Also remember that keeping your emotions in check is crucial for your future success with any type of investing that you participate in. You want to avoid falling into the same trap that so many do and sell or buy an investment when emotions are high. Have a financial advisor in your corner to help you rationalize and navigate these periods of high emotions is important.

As Warren Buffett says, *"Be fearful when others are greedy and greedy when others are fearful."* When the inevitable happens

123

and the world seems to go to hell in a handbasket that's when you want to have money waiting to invest. The problem is, to take advantages of opportunities like this you need to have some cash on the sidelines ready and waiting to deploy. That's what an opportunity fund is for. An opportunity fund is money that you set aside so that when an opportunity arises, you have the money to take advantage of it. This is very important to consider because most of the growth you get in any market is during a recovery phase after a correction takes place. A correction is a decline in an investment market of at least 10% from its 52-week high. While no one can predict a market correction, we can look to past events to help anticipate when the next correction in a market might be coming. In the case of a market correction, you can use your opportunity fund to buy stocks, bonds, real estate, or other investments at reduced prices! The size of an opportunity fund is based on personal preference and there is no wrong size. The more pessimistic you feel about an investment market, the more you may want to contribute to an opportunity fund. Your opportunity fund, like all money that you plan to use in the short term, should be kept in a safe and easily accessible place such as a savings account or money market fund.

Despite all the risks mentioned above, investing can make you money over the long term if you approach it in the right manner, understand the investment, and can keep your emotions out of it. I had mentioned above, even accounting for the down years, the overall average return of the S&P 500 is still 8% annually. Proper asset allocation and diversification are how you mitigate the risks of investing. After all, the real risk is not investing your money at all.

Investing is all about your understanding of the investment markets you are looking to enter, your time horizon to take on the investments, and the level of risk with each investment that you're comfortable taking on. It's important to have a professional such as a financial advisor there to help guide you on what investments best meet your specific goals and needs. Investing can be one of the best ways to grow your wealth and secure your future paycheck but the longer you wait to get started, the harder it is to catch up. By the year 2033, it is estimated that almost 40% of American jobs will be lost to automation[46]. This reinforces why you can't rely on working

---

[46] PwC Report, March 2017

for a paycheck your entire life. Many people always search for the answers on how to become a millionaire, but building wealth isn't about learning a few financial secrets and tips. There is no such thing as "getting rich quickly". Investing is about long-term commitment to saving and making wise investment choices to help build your wealth. It may not be sexy, but it works. I hope I've helped you realize how important it is to stop waiting to invest and motivated you to start putting money away TODAY, to create your future paycheck.

Exercise 4:
Investment Goals

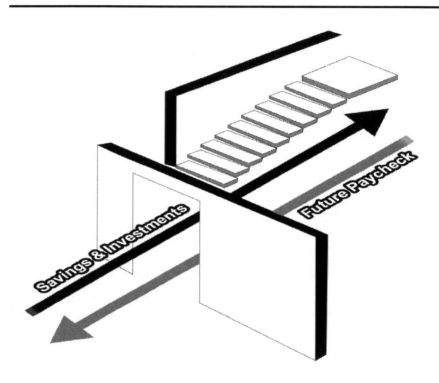

Your investments represent your money going up the stairs in your financial home to rest in the bedroom and grow, one day coming back down the steps to your first floor in the form of a future paycheck when you retire.

Let's answer a few questions on the following pages about your current level of knowledge around investing and any current investments and contributions you have towards them. There're no right or wrong answers to these questions. Let these questions and your answers serve as a baseline to test your current level of understanding around investing so that you can start to make a positive change in your investments going forward.

1. What is your current investment knowledge?

    a. Non-existent to extremely limited – you have never invested before and have almost no current understanding as to how investing works.

    b. Fair – you have invested before (retirement, etc.), have some basic knowledge, and are familiar with the difference between stocks and bonds.

    c. Good – you have a solid understanding around investment markets and how various investments work.

    d. Excellent – you have an in-depth understanding around investments and understand the risks and rewards associated when investing in various investment markets and types.

2. Do you have any current investment accounts setup? How much of your monthly income are you contributing towards investing for your future?

3. For any investments that you have, do you know and understand what your current asset allocation is? What do you have invested between stocks, bonds, mutual funds, ETFs, real estate, cash, or any other investments?

4. Does your employer offer any type of retirement plan such as a 401(k)? If so, do you currently contribute towards it? What is the maximum match that your employer's retirement plan offers and are you taking advantage of this free money? What is the current asset allocation of the account?

5. If you own your own business, have you created any sort of retirement plan for yourself and any employees? If so, how much are you currently contributing towards it? What is the current asset allocation of the account?

6. How much of temporary decrease (for example one year) in the value of your investments could you tolerate?
   a. No decrease
   b. Less than 5% decrease
   c. 5% to 10% decrease
   d. 10% to 15% decrease
   e. More than 15% decrease

7. When making investment decisions, you are:
   a. Conservative and try to minimize your risk
   b. Conservative but willing to accept a small amount of risk
   c. Moderate with the amount of risk you're willing to accept
   d. Somewhat aggressive and take on some larger risks
   e. Aggressive and typically take on large risks

8. Your investments need to:
   a. Be readily available for emergencies or short-term needs
   b. Be reasonably secure and safe from short-term loses
   c. Generate a steady stream of income
   d. Generate some income with some opportunity to grow in value
   e. Generate long-term growth
   f. Aggressively grow in value

If you don't know the answer to any of these questions, or if you have yet to begin investing towards your future, the first step is to educate yourself on any retirement accounts that pertain to you and about any investments that you would consider utilizing. I recommend that you consult with a financial advisor before you begin investing to ensure you're taking advantage of the proper investment accounts and using the right asset allocation that fits your needs, to create your future paycheck.

"Money is multiplied in practical value depending on the number of W's you control in your life: what you do, when you do it, where you do it, and with whom you do it"

Timothy Ferriss

Chapter 9

Living Off Your Investments

Now that you know the steps you must take to build your future paycheck, it's time to create a plan for spending that future paycheck in a manner that it doesn't run out. For this, we will use the 4% rule which is a simple formula for calculating your retirement. This is how you can determine how much money you must invest and what rate of return you must achieve on your investments so that your money works for you when you no longer wish to work. The 4% rule can be used to calculate how much money you are able to withdraw from your investment accounts during retirement, every year, for at least thirty years without depleting those accounts and outliving your money. With the 4% rule there are no complicated formulas involved and even someone who has no understanding of finance can understand how to use the rule as a basis for their retirement planning.

Here's how the 4% rule works. You should aim to withdraw no more than 4% of your investments in any one year during your retirement. If you have $1,000,000 saved upon your retirement, you would withdraw and live on $40,000 each year from your investments. If you'd like to live on $80,000 a year during your retirement, you can easily determine how much you must have saved upon retirement. On your calculator take $80,000 and divide it by .04. This gives you $2,000,000. So, if you wish to live on $80,000 a year during retirement, you ideally would want to have at least $2,000,000 saved up upon your retirement. Give this a try yourself, what's comfortable amount annual income that you feel you could live on during retirement? Take that number and divide by .04. Does the number shock you? Do you have a plan on how to reach that number?

In retirement you still need to account for inflation, so you would want to increase the amount of your first year's withdrawal of $80,000 in subsequent years to reflect the impact inflation has on the purchasing power of your money.

If the average annual inflation rate in our country is 3%, in the second year of your retirement you would look to take out $82,400 ($80,000 + 3% inflation). This calculation is done by taking your desired annual withdrawal of $80,000 and multiplying it by 1.03 (3%). The next year you would withdraw $84,872 ($82,400 + 3% inflation) and so on. You would continue the 4% withdrawal along with the extra amount each year, to preserve the purchasing power of your money against inflation no matter what the investment markets are doing or how your portfolio is performing.

Adding in the extra amounts to account for inflation will help your money to retain the same purchasing power throughout your retirement. When in retirement, if your investments can average an annual rate of return of 4% (your withdrawal rate) plus the annual rate of inflation, you would be able to live on the annual growth of your investments without dipping into your principal, allowing you to continue your lifestyle without the worry of running out of money indefinitely. This however, is easier said than done as no one can predict what the future may hold for any investment. As such, the 4% rule is just a guide to help you estimate your target amount of savings and investments upon retirement. After you've determined your target savings and investment amounts upon retirement, you can begin to look at what you must start saving and investing today, along with what rate of return you must achieve annually to achieve that target amount.

The most important variable is having enough money saved for retirement. If you only have $100,000 saved for retirement, and you apply the 4% rule, you would be living on $4,000 a year which is simply not realistic. People are living longer than ever, and our money must outlive us, otherwise it's game over. While none of us can know how long we'll live or how much we'll spend in retirement, there are some ways to estimate.

By now you should have your budget identified and be able to analyze what your monthly income, expenses, savings, and investments are. This will be critical to help you estimate what your retirement income needs could be, how much you need to be saving and investing each month, and what rate of return you must achieve annually to meet those future needs today. To get a starting point for what your expenses *could be* in retirement, I want you to look at your current monthly expenses.

Take the total of your current monthly expenses and multiply it by 12 to give you your estimated annual expenses. Now you need to estimate what effect inflation will have on your expenses each year going forward, to get an idea of how much your expenses might increase by the time you enter retirement.

To calculate the effect of inflation on your current expenses over the next year, take your current annual expenses and multiply them by 1.0x. Let x represent any amount you wish to use for inflation. If you want to assume annual inflation is 3%, you would multiply by 1.03. Assuming your current annual expenses are $30,000 and annual inflation is 3%, by next year your expenses will increase to $30,900 ($30,000 x 1.03). This means that in the course of one year, your monthly expenses could rise by $900 and while that doesn't sound terrible, think in terms of 30 or 40 years when you're ready to retire. How much will your expenses today cost in retirement?

This can easily be calculated on your smartphone by downloading a financial calculator app. There are quite a few free financial calculator apps available for use, one that I use often is EZ Financial Calculators. You'll need to understand the functions of the calculator, so let me give you a brief tutorial on how to use the calculator to solve this equation. I will be referencing the EZ Financial Calculators app in my examples so keep in mind that other financial calculator apps may have a different home screen to navigate. The functions of any financial calculator will be the same. You can also find this calculator online at www.fncalculator.com.

Upon downloading and opening EZ Financial Calculators, find the TVM Calculator. TVM stands for Time Value of Money. The time value of money concept states that money available at the present time is worth more than the identical amount in the future, due to its potential earning capacity. This can hold true for money that is invested and earning a certain rate of return, or expenses that are increasing in cost due to inflation. The most fundamental TVM formula uses the following variables:

PV: This means present value. It's the current amount of any investments or the total of any expenses.

PMT: This means payment. It's the amount that you're adding to the present value (PV) per compounding period (daily, weekly, monthly, etc.). This could be contributions into a retirement account such as a 401(k) or IRA, contributions into a non-qualified investment account, or savings into a bank account.

FV: This is your future value. If you're trying to calculate what the present value of your money will be worth in the future once you've made any additional payments and let compound interest work its magic, you'll see your answer here.

Rate: This is the rate of growth. This would be the rate of return on an investment or the rate of inflation. If you assume an investment would grow by 7%, enter 7. If you assume inflation will grow by 3% enter 3.

Periods: This is the number of times you're compounding your money whether it be daily, weekly, monthly, etc.

Let's look at the same example we calculated above. I want you to follow along on your financial calculator. Assuming your current annual expenses are $30,000 and annual inflation is 3%, what would your expenses increase to by next year? Enter the following into your financial calculator:

PV: 30,000
PMT: 0
Rate: 3
Periods: 1
Compounding: make sure it is set to annual
FV: hit the FV button to solve the equation

In the FV box you should see -30,900. The reason this is a negative number is that it represents future cash outflows of $30,900.

Now let's look at what your expenses may look like 30 years from now. Let's assume your current annual expenses are $30,000, you wish to retire in 30 years, and annual inflation will be 3%. On your financial calculator input the following:

PV: 30,000
PMT: 0
Rate: 3
Periods: 30
Compounding: make sure it is set to annual
FV: hit the FV button to solve the equation

In the FV box you should see -72,817.87. That means if your expenses grow with an annual inflation of 3%, in 30 years your expenses will be $72,817.87 for the same stuff!

Will inflation be less extreme over the next 30 years? Will it be even more extreme? No one knows, but it's wise to begin preparing for your future today so that you can ensure your paycheck is enough to cover all your expenses in the future.

When consider your estimated retirement expenses, you also need to ask yourself where you would want to spend your retirement? Would it be in the same potentially high cost living area that you're currently located, or would you move to an area with a much lower cost of living? Would you do the opposite and move to an even higher cost of living area, maybe somewhere by the beach? Will you pay off your home before you retire, or will you sell your home and downgrade to a smaller one or maybe rent rather than deal with the hassles of home ownership during your retirement? If you have a family or plan to have one someday, do you want to leave them an inheritance or do you want the last check you write to bounce?

How will you invest your money? Investing in stocks for your retirement portfolio provides potential for future growth to help support your spending needs later in retirement. Bonds and cash on the other hand can add stability to your portfolio and can be used to fund your early needs in retirement. Real estate investing can potentially provide a second form of income to further help support your retirement paycheck. Each investment serves its own role, so a good mix whether it be stocks, bonds, real estate, or cash, is important.

Your asset allocation has a significant impact on your investment portfolio's ending balance. A more aggressive investment portfolio has the potential to grow more over time, but the drawback is that in down years the portfolio will perform worse than a more conservative investment portfolio. Picking an investment allocation that you're comfortable with, especially in the event of a bear market and not just the one with the greatest possibility to increase in potential value is key. Working with a financial advisor will help to ensure that your investment allocation always meets your specific needs and that when those needs change, so does your investment allocation.

Will you continue to work in some capacity during retirement, maybe part-time or as a consultant? Remember, retirement doesn't have to mean the end of work; it just means the end of mandatory work or a work optional lifestyle as I like to call it. These are all important questions to ask yourself so that you can best prepare for your retirement. Once you can answer these questions, you can begin to estimate what your income needs will be during your retirement and what you must be saving and investing today to meet those needs.

Let's look at the flip side of this coin, calculating what you must save and invest towards retirement. Remember, it's easy to determine a number that you would wish to be able to live on each year in retirement, however you need to take it one step further to determine what you must begin saving and investing today, to reach that goal.

Let's look at a husband and wife, both at the age of 30, earning a combined gross income of $100,000 annually, and who wish to retire at the age of 60. Their annual net income is $78,000. Let's assume that until now they have not contributed any of their income towards saving and investing for their future. If they decided to invest 20% of their net income each year going forward (assuming their income remains the same with no raises) and feel that they can attain an annual rate of return of 8%, how much could they spend per year in retirement? Let's head back to our financial calculators to find out. Enter the following on your financial calculator:

PV: 0
PMT: -1,300
Rate: 8
Periods: 360
Compounding: make sure it is set to monthly
FV: hit the FV button to solve the equation

In the FV box you should see 1,937,467.28. This couple has the potential to have $1,937,467.28 saved up upon their retirement. If they follow the 4% rule they would be able to live on about $77,500 each year during their retirement.

So how did I get these numbers? First, I started by looking at their net annual income of $78,000. We need to determine what 20% of that income is that they can direct towards saving and investing. On your calculator you would take $78,000 x .20 to determine what 20% of their net income would be, which in this case is $15,600. Next you would divide $15,600 by 12 to determine what they should look to save and invest each month, so in this case it's $1,300. When entering $1,300 into PMT it would be a negative number since they're directing money "out" of their cash inflows towards savings and investments. For periods, you would need to look at how many months they'll be contributing $1,300 towards savings and investments. In this case it would be 360 months, or 30 years x 12 contributions each year. Lastly you would want to make sure that compounding is also set to monthly to reflect the monthly contribution.

This is a very important and helpful calculation to know and understand, as it gives you a basic understanding if you're on track for retirement or not. For the same couple, lets look at the effects of a higher or lower rate of return on their investments and how this affects their future spending potential with all other variables remaining the same.

If the couple were able to achieve an annual rate of return of 10%, let's look at how their retirement picture might look. Enter the following on your financial calculator:

PV: 0
PMT: -1,300
Rate: 10
Periods: 360
Compounding: make sure it is set to monthly
FV: hit the FV button to solve the equation

In the FV box you should see 2,938,634.30. If their investments achieve an annual rate of return of 10%, the couple has the potential to have $2,938,634.30 saved up upon their retirement. If they follow the 4% rule, they would be able to live on about $117,500 each year during their retirement, not too shabby!

If the couple were able to achieve an annual rate of return of only 4%, let's look at how their retirement picture might look. Enter the following on your financial calculator:

PV: 0
PMT: -1,300
Rate: 4
Periods: 360
Compounding: make sure it is set to monthly
FV: hit the FV button to solve the equation

In the FV box you should see 902,264.23. If their investments achieve an annual rate of return of 4%, the couple has the potential to have $902,264.23 saved up upon their retirement. If they follow the 4% rule, they would be able to live on about $36,000 each year during their retirement. This is dramatically different than the previous examples!

I want these examples to show you not only the importance of saving and investing for your future as soon as possible, but also the importance of a properly managed investment portfolio. Working with a financial advisor to ensure that you hit your savings and investment goals along with maintaining an investment portfolio to meet your needs is crucial.

A fun thing about this exercise is that you can apply it to anything you want to find the future value of. You could use this to determine anticipated future costs such as a wedding, school costs, buying a house or car, or anything else you want to save for over time.

Let's look at an example where you wish to purchase a $300,000 home in 2 years, where property prices in the area are increasing on average about 7% annually. What would the $300,000 home cost you in 2 years? Enter the following on your financial calculator:

PV: 300,000
PMT: 0
Rate: 7
Periods: 2
Compounding: make sure it is set to annual
FV: hit the FV button to solve the equation

In the FV box you should see -343,470. In 2 years, the same home will cost you $343,470 if property prices on average increase by 7% annually.

Often, people's lifestyle and expenses directly correlate to where they live and the property that they live on. When looking at where you wish to live, you should consider a few things to ensure that you don't overextend yourself prior to or during your retirement. There's a simple formula to follow that you can use to determine what your income, savings, and investing must look like to afford the property that you're living on as well as the lifestyle that will come with it. Not preparing for this is one reason you often hear of someone "downsizing" their home in retirement. They potentially failed to plan for the ongoing expenses of the home and their lifestyle and now need to cut back their lifestyle and expenses to avoid running out of money.

To figure this out for yourself, think of the home, condo, or apartment that you would wish to live in as well as the area that you wish to live in and determine the cost. This applies whether you will own the property or will be renting it. Take the value of that property and divide it by 30% (.30). This will give you your minimum net annual income that you need to support your lifestyle pre-retirement. Next multiply that income by 4% (.04) to see how much money you would need to have saved upon your retirement so that you could continue your lifestyle without the worry of running out of money.

For a 1-million-dollar home, you would need at least $300,000 of net annual income to support your lifestyle in your years before retirement ($1,000,000 x .03) and you would need $7,500,000 ($300,000/.04) of savings and investments upon your retirement to maintain this lifestyle with a 4% withdrawal rate. If this is your goal, are you saving enough? Is the rate of return on your investment currently enough to reach this goal? These are all important things to ask yourself and review on a routine basis to ensure that whatever your goals are, you meet them.

The 4% rule should not be the only basis of your retirement plan because it's too inflexible and too dependent on economic conditions that no one can guarantee. The 4% rule is, however, a good starting place if you have no idea where to start when it comes to understanding how much you will need for retirement.

There are several scenarios in which the 4% rule might not work for your retirement planning. If your investment portfolio features higher-risk investments than typical stocks, bonds, or real estate, you may need to be more conservative when withdrawing money, particularly during the early years of retirement. A severe investment market downturn can erode the value of high-risk investments much faster than it can a typical retirement portfolio. This rule will also not work unless you remain loyal to it continually in retirement. Violating the rule one year to splurge on a big purchase and spending beyond the 4% withdrawal rate, can have major consequences down the road as you may dip into your investments principal and affect the ability for compound interest to do its job.

The 4% rule should be used as a starting point, a basic guideline on how much to save for retirement to know what you can spend in retirement. The eventual transition from saving towards to spending your investments can be challenging. There will never be a one size fits all answer to how much you can spend from your investments in retirement. What's important is that you have a plan and a general guideline for spending and then adjust as needed. Your goal, after all, is to enjoy your retirement. Now you should have a good idea of how your investments can pay you in the future as well as how you can maintain a lifestyle that you can afford.

"Your story is the greatest legacy that you will leave to your friends. It's the longest-lasting legacy you will leave to your heirs."

Steve Saint

Chapter 10

Your Life, Your Legacy

When most people think of financial planning, they think of paying down debt, saving money, building their investments, and planning for retirement. While those are all important aspects of financial planning there is another aspect that is greatly overlooked, especially for younger people, and that's insurance and estate planning.

Insurance and estate planning complete the construction of your financial home by acting as the roof over your head, offering protection from the unknown. Insurance and estate planning allow you to have the proper insurance coverage and legal documentation in place, protecting you and your family in the event of an illness, accident, or untimely death. It's important for everyone to have coverage like this, especially millennials. As a millennial, one of the last things you're probably thinking about is insurance and estate planning, and the biggest obstacle is the misconception that insurance and estate planning are only for older or wealthier individuals. If you don't have kids, don't own a home, or don't have any major assets, it may be easy for you to dismiss the importance of estate planning, but you know what they say about making assumptions, right?

When I first meet with my clients, whether they're millennials or not, I notice that the most neglected area of their financial plan is proper insurance and estate planning. Married or single, young or old, parents of two kids or dog parents, not having proper insurance and estate planning documents is a mistake. Insurance planning is designed to protect you, your loved ones, your home, your assets, and your business against unexpected events. Insurance is designed to help ease financial burdens that can occur when the unknown happens. Estate planning involves planning for how your assets will be preserved, managed, and distributed after your death. It also considers the management of your properties and financial obligations if you become incapacitated. Assets that could make up your estate include a house, car, stocks or other investments, life insurance, or a 401(k). There are many reasons for insurance and estate planning, such as providing for your surviving spouse and children, funding your child's future education, or leaving your legacy behind to a charitable cause.

Even though no one likes to think about things like death and disability, planning for these events ahead of time can make life much easier for ourselves and our loved ones in the event of a worst-case scenario. While it may sound like an exhausting process, the truth is you don't need much to start planning. In fact, the less you own, the easier the process will be. Here are a few reasons why, even as a millennial, insurance and estate planning should be a priority.

Insurance planning is a critical component to financial planning and includes evaluating current and unknown risks present in your life and determining the proper insurance coverage to mitigate those risks. The main goal of insurance planning is to identify and analyze risk factors in your life and seek proper coverage to have peace of mind if disaster strikes. Insurance is a contract, represented by a policy, in which a person receives financial protection or reimbursement against losses from an insurance company. There are many different forms of insurance to protect you and your estate such as health insurance, auto and home insurance, disability insurance, and life insurance. It's important to work with a financial advisor to help you choose the appropriate insurance coverage based on your individual situation.

Carrying insurance is crucial, but the most important aspect is carrying the appropriate type of insurance. Everyone has different insurance needs tied to their unique situation like their age, their health, their family structure, and their economic status. There are several forms of insurance and there is no one size fits all approach. To determine on the type of insurance you need for your unique life situation, you should research with a financial advisor what types of insurance are available in today's market.

Being a millennial you're probably as healthy as you'll ever be, and you're as young as you'll ever be. Does this mean that you should ignore health insurance? Absolutely not. Even healthy people can develop ailments, catch diseases, and get into accidents. The upside as a young and healthy person, is that you'll find the cost of buying insurance to be more affordable than it is for older Americans. Health insurance is usually available through your employer, but this is not always the case. If not, you will have to seek private insurance. It's critical that you have health insurance for you and your family to match your risk tolerance and medical needs. Keep in mind, the cheaper the plan you find, the more constraints there may be. You need to evaluate and understand each plan that is offered to you prior to making a final decision. By going without health insurance, you take a gamble on your health with the assumption that it will stay good, but what happens to you and your finances if that changes?

Disability insurance is a type of insurance that will provide you income if you're unable to perform your work and earn money due to a disability. Most employers offer some type of disability coverage. It's important to make sure that if your employer offers disability coverage, you consider taking advantage of it, even if it's an added expense. Each employer disability insurance policy has specific rules as to what constitutes a disability and how you might qualify to receive the disability benefit. Short term disability insurance offers you a portion of your salary (typically 40-60%) if you're unable to work for a short period of time (typically 3-6 months). Long term disability insurance offers you a portion of your salary (typically 50-70%) if you're unable to work for a longer period (typically over 6 months). Both short term and long term disability policies have a required period of time that you must be disabled before you are eligible to receive disability benefits. This required period of time is called an elimination period. If you become disabled, you must wait until the elimination period is over before you can receive any benefits. If your employer does not offer disability insurance, you can purchase an individual policy from an insurance agent.

An individual disability policy gives you more options in terms of shorter elimination periods, longer benefit periods, and optional protection plans such as critical illness or hospital confinement. When you're buying an individual policy, you should know that it can be expensive, so in some cases you may be better off building a strong emergency fund instead of purchasing a disability policy. Some long term disability insurance policies offer a student loan rider in which your student loans would be paid if you were to become disabled. An insurance rider is an adjustment to an insurance policy for a small fee that provides an additional benefit over what is described in the basic policy. If you have student loan debt, I would consider adding this rider to your policy.

A home and car are likely to be the most expensive purchases you will make, and insurance is needed not only to protect these assets, but it's also required by the terms of your loan to protect the creditors (the bank) in case of a loss or need for replacement. Owners as well as renters can get insurance to cover the contents of their home. You need to do your research and find enough coverage to protect your assets according to your personal situation. Keep in mind that every state has financial responsibility laws that require you to pay for any liabilities that you may cause in an accident. An umbrella insurance policy is extra insurance coverage that goes beyond the limits of your home or auto policy and provides an additional layer of security in case you're sued for damages to other people's property or injuries caused to others in an accident.

Many millennials have started their own businesses or work in family businesses. If you're self-employed, you would need to cover not only yourself and your family, but also your business. There are many options available to you after you decide which risks you need to insure. Business insurance protects your small business from financial damages that can result from accidents, property damage, errors, workers' compensation claims, and other situations. Having the adequate business insurance as well as a business plan will protect your business in the event you pass away or become incapacitated. This is important, so your business can retain its value and provide certainty for customers and employees. Having a plan and the appropriate coverage is critical in minimizing the risk to your business. As a business owner, you need to understand the value of protecting your intellectual property so be sure to protect yourself and what you've built.

Life insurance should be part of your financial plan and is a great way to ensure your family can continue to live the life you intended for them if you pass away unexpectedly. Life insurance is critical for individuals with family members to protect upon one's loss of life. A surviving spouse, children, or other dependents can use the funds to maintain their standard of living, protect loss of assets, or repay any remaining debt. The amount you would need is dependent upon your family situation and what you aim to protect. A great rule of thumb is that if you're single, you should consider having enough life insurance to cover all your outstanding liabilities. If you're married, consider having enough life insurance to not only cover all your household's outstanding liabilities, but also enough to replace your loss of income so that your spouse does not need to adjust their standard of living. If you're married with children, you should further consider the cost of raising each child and any higher education costs that they may incur. There are two types of life insurance I want to focus on, term life and whole life.

Term life insurance is life insurance that guarantees payment of a stated death benefit during a specified term. The death benefit is the amount of money the insurance company guarantees to the beneficiaries identified in your policy upon your death. Once the term expires, you either renew for another term, convert to permanent coverage (whole life), or allow the policy to terminate. Term life insurance has no value other than the guaranteed death benefit. There is no savings component as is found in a whole life insurance policy. Term life insurance premiums are typically lower than whole life insurance premiums because the policy only offers a benefit for a stated period of time. If you were to die within the specified policy term, the insurance company will pay the value of the policy to your beneficiaries. Should the policy expire before your death, there is no payout. There are many types of term life insurance, the most popular being level term. Level term life insurance provides coverage for a specified period ranging from 10 to 30 years. Term life insurance policies are ideal for people who want substantial coverage at low costs.

Whole life insurance provides coverage for your entire life. In addition to providing a death benefit, whole life insurance also contains a savings component where a cash value may grow. These policies are also known as permanent life insurance. Whole life insurance guarantees payment of a death benefit to your beneficiaries in exchange for regular premium payments. The policy includes a savings portion, called the cash value, alongside the death benefit. In the savings component, interest may accumulate on a tax-deferred basis. Growing cash value is an important part of whole life insurance. The cash value offers a benefit to you, the policyholder. The cash value serves as a source of equity. To access the cash value, you would request a withdrawal of funds or a loan. You may withdraw funds tax-free up to the value of total premiums paid. Withdrawals reduce the cash value but not the death benefit of your policy. Loans will reduce your policy's death benefit by the amount you are withdrawing. The death benefit of a whole life insurance policy is typically a set amount of the policy contract. Some policies are eligible for dividend payments. In this case, the policyholder (you) may elect to have the dividends purchase additional death benefits, which will increase the death benefit at the time of your death. Many insurers offer riders that protect the death benefit if you, the insured, become disabled or become critically or terminally ill.

Group life insurance is offered by an employer or other large-scale entities, such as an association, to its employees or members. This type of life insurance is usually inexpensive or even free and has a relatively low death benefit amount. It is typically offered as a piece of a larger employer or membership benefit package. If your employer offers group life insurance, you may not have to pay anything out of pocket for the policy benefits, or you may elect to have the premium payment deducted from your paycheck. The most common type of group life insurance is term life insurance.

As a millennial, you probably feel your life is just beginning, and the ending is too far off to even consider. We still feel youthful and have a sense of immortality. We carry the assumption that estate planning is just for older people or have the belief that we don't need estate planning as it's too far away in the future. A recent survey found that 78% of Americans under the age of 36 don't have any estate documents in place[47]. Unfortunately, we never know when our time will be up but having an estate plan in place will

---

[47] Caring.com 2017 Study

allow you to enjoy your life knowing your family and your assets will be taken care of. We need to understand how important it is for us to take control of our future and begin to plan for the unforeseen as well as the inevitable.

If you're like most millennials, you're probably thinking to yourself *"What assets? I don't own any property or have anything to distribute if anything was to happen to me."* While that may be true to an extent, there are some other things you need to think about like your job. Have you established a retirement plan such as a 401(k) and does your employer offer life insurance? What about your personal property? Do you own a car or have any home furnishings that may be worth any value? Without an estate plan, what happens to these items will be left for the State and the Court system to decide. This means that your assets could potentially end up in the hands of someone other than who you intend. Estate planning is the preparation of tasks and documents that serve to manage your assets in the event of your incapacitation or death. It's basically a process to organize your affairs so that if you were unable to care for yourself or worse, you pass away, your financial house would be in order and not a burden to your family members.

Your last will and testament are documents that dictate how you want your assets distributed upon your death. This document will also appoint an executor to oversee the settling of your estate. A will only goes into effect after your death and after it passes through probate. Probate is when a court oversees the administration of your will, ensuring it's valid and that your assets and personal property go to those named in your will. Without this document, the state will take over the handling of your assets, personal property, and even decide who has guardianship of any children you may have, should their other parent also be deceased or otherwise not able or willing to care for them.

Assets that should be addressed are any employer retirement accounts that you contribute towards, any life insurance policies that you have, any real estate or vehicles you own, and any other tangible assets like family memorabilia, pets, and digital assets. Digital assets are an area of growing importance. Estate planning documents should address digital assets such as content on your social media accounts, apps, electronically-stored data, airline points, loyalty programs, financial accounts, photos, and videos.

Millennials might wish to designate a "digital executor" to manage these accounts and provide instructions about what to do with them. For example, to memorialize a Facebook account you may wish for someone to delete any embarrassing photos and videos. It would be wise to prepare a detailed list of your accounts, user names, and passwords so that a person you trust, or your executor can gain access to these accounts. You can store this information and important estate planning documents in online document storage clouds or in a safe. It doesn't matter what your financial situation is, you need a will.

When we're young there's a tendency to think that you'll live forever, but what if you do become incapacitated? This could be caused by an injury on the job or an automobile accident that leaves you incapable of taking care of yourself and ultimately, your expenses. If you're near death or in a persistent vegetative state, a living will communicates what type of medical care, life-sustaining or resuscitation efforts, and pain medications you wish to receive. I recommended you also consider the follow documents:

HIPAA Authorization: If you ever find yourself in the hospital, this document gives authorization for doctors and medical professionals to discuss your condition with anyone of your choosing.

Power of Attorney for Health Care: This allows a designated person to make life or death decisions on your health care when you cannot.

"Durable" Financial Power of Attorney: A typical Power of Attorney (POA) designation ends at your incapacity, however a "durable" power of attorney remains in place through your incapacitation and gives a designated person legal authority to manage your finances without court interference. A durable power of attorney states who can make financial decisions for you if you are no longer able to do things like pay bills or manage your assets. This person should be someone you really trust.

Health Care Proxy: This allows a designated person to make medical decisions for you. This person should know what your wishes are in advance, should the occasion arise.

You should seriously consider routinely reviewing your will and other estate documents to ensure everything listed in them is still as you wish. You should also consider routinely reviewing all account beneficiaries. You want to ensure that only those that you name as beneficiaries will continue to receive your assets and personal property. Check your beneficiaries on prior and current 401(k) accounts as well as any other retirement accounts, all investment accounts, and all bank accounts. This is important because beneficiaries listed on accounts take precedent over what is listed in your will.

Being wealthy is not a requirement for creating an estate plan, neither is being old, retired, having a family, or owning a lot of assets. As a millennial, if you haven't started estate planning, you should do so now. Consider working with an estate planning attorney who knows the federal and state laws that apply to your situation. There is some work you should do before meeting with an attorney, like making a list of all your current assets and what you would want done with them. This includes bank accounts, vehicles, and that Beanie Baby collection your parents thought was going to fund your retirement. If you have children, decide who will be their guardian or caretaker and decide who will control your finances.

As the saying goes, there are only two things in like that are certain- death and taxes. With the being said, planning for these events should be done no matter how young or old you are and regardless of how much stuff you think you have. Coming to terms with the passing of a loved one is enough of a burden and what many of us millennials don't realize is the mountain of tasks and decisions our families face in the event of our incapacity or death. I hope that I've helped to educate you on the importance of insurance and estate planning to help take the pressure off your family members in the future.

Exercise 5:
Are You Protected from the Unknown?

Insurance & Estate Planning

The roof over your financial home is put into place when you established a plan for protection from the unknown, such as having the appropriate type and amount of insurance coverage and all your estate documents created.

Let's answer a few questions on the following pages around your current insurance coverage and any estate documents that you have in place. As with the previous exercise, there're no right or wrong answers to these questions.

1. Do you have health insurance in place whether it's through your employer or an exchange?

2. Do you have disability coverage in place in the event you're injured and unable to perform your job? Is this type of insurance offered through your employer?

3. What type and amount, if any, of life insurance do you have in place? Does your employer offer any life insurance coverage?

   Remember the simple rule: If you're single, you should consider having enough life insurance to cover all your outstanding liabilities. If you're married, consider having enough life insurance to not only cover all your household's outstanding liabilities, but also enough to replace your loss of income so that your spouse does not need to adjust their standard of living. If you're married with children, you should further consider the cost of raising each child and any higher education costs that they may incur.

4. Do you have a last will and testament in place? Have you given any thought as to what would happen to your assets or personal property if you were to pass away unexpectedly? Write a list down of whom you would like things to go to. If you have children, do you have written arrangements for who will care for them in case something was to happen to you and the child's other parent?

   For any digital assets that you own, do you have a list of all account usernames and passwords for someone that you trust to access?

5. Do you have a HIPAA Authorization, Power of Attorney for Health Care, "Durable" Financial Power of Attorney, or a Health Care Proxy created?

If you do not have any insurance or estate documents in place, it would be wise to work with a financial advisor and an estate planning attorney to ensure that you have adequate coverage and proper documents in place now before it's too late. One thing's for certain, and that is that never know what can happen in the future. It's always good to plan and prepare for the unexpected.

"The mind has a powerful way of attracting things that are in harmony with it, good and bad."

Idowu Koyenikan

Chapter 11

Creating Your Mindset

How often have you thought that if you just had a million dollars, you'd be happy? Maybe you've pondered how you could save $20,000 for the car that you want or even $1,000 for the handbag you desire. We've all had those thoughts at some point. Your bank account, investing strategy, and career aren't the only important parts of your financial life and your net worth and rate of return on your investments aren't the most pivotal aspects either. The most important aspect of your financial life is your mindset. Without the right mindset around your financial well-being, those other metrics of success amount to nothing. A healthy mindset leads to productive behaviors and a positive relationship with your money. Without this foundational approach to managing your financial life, no amount of planning and execution can improve your situation.

The problem with this is that all the statements above come from the wrong mindset. Many people focus on having more, more, more, but how many of them execute the actions that get the money and financial freedom they desire? I've already explained how money allows you the ability to be free and how it's what gets you that freedom from debt, freedom to retire, and peace of mind for the future, but your mindset is an equally important part of those goals.

Your mindset dictates your outcome in life with anything that you do. If you have a positive mindset about something, you're more likely to see it through and complete the task. If you have a negative mindset about something, your probability of success for that task drops significantly. If you have a poor mindset about money, money management, and financial planning, this can lead to a poor financial life. Having a positive mindset though doesn't necessarily mean good things will happen overnight, it just means that you'll be more likely to take the necessary action to achieve what you want. Think about what you are willing to give up right now to get what you want in the future. Are you willing to give up your weekends with friends to work a second job to pay off debt and begin to create a future paycheck? Are you willing to give up your current vehicle for a more affordable one if it puts you in a better financial position for the future?

Two great examples that show a terrible mindset with money are the two people we discussed earlier, MC Hammer and Jim Hayes. MC Hammer who once had a net worth of over 33 million dollars, allowed his poor mindset with money to burn through his fortune, which caused him to end up in bankruptcy. Jim Hayes won a $19 million-dollar lottery only to end up in a mountain of debt where he resorted to robbing banks just to survive. Both men had a very poor mindset around money and ultimately, that mindset led them to squander all the money and wealth they once had.

A healthy financial mindset is like going to the gym. Personally, I enjoy the gym and maintaining an overall healthy physique and lifestyle. But do you know what I hate about the gym? The month of January, when all over the nation, people with New Year's Resolutions descend upon their local gym, causing the rest of us to sprint in from the parking lot to stake our claim on the gym equipment. The New Year's Resolution people walk around like zombies, like the White Walkers descending upon Winterfell (for all you Game of Thrones lovers). Then suddenly when March arrives, just like the White Walkers and the plot of the entire 8th season of Game of Thrones, they disappear. Why is it that so many people make a resolution for this commitment every year but never stick with it or follow through? The answer is simple – their mindset.

Most people aren't specific enough when they formulate a goal and that greatly hinders their probability of success. Their goals are very vague like wanting to look good in a bathing suit, lose weight, or get in better shape. Those goals aren't clear enough and what they should be doing is defining the specifics of what it means to look good in a bathing suit, to lose weight, and to get in better shape. The problem here is that these goals lack clarity and will hinder your ability to reach them because you have no specific goal to aim for. It's like going hunting without a scope on your rifle and expecting to hit a target that's over 100 yards away.

If you tell yourself you want to lose weight but don't specify the number of pounds you would like to drop, how can you know what you need to do to lose that weight? If you don't weigh yourself before you start, how do you even know where you stand? The same holds true with financial planning. If you say you want to be wealthy, pay off your debt, or retire comfortably, but don't sit down and figure out details for each goal, how will you ever achieve them? If your goal is to become debt free, you need to look at how much debt you currently have, how much of your current cash flow you can put towards paying down your debt each month, and how long it would take you to become debt free. If you want to have a comfortable retirement, you need to look at how much money you're currently saving and investing for your retirement, when you plan to retire, how much income you'll need at retirement, and if you're currently saving enough to create a realistic paycheck for yourself in retirement. If you aren't being specific, your probability of success is going to be very low.

When you no longer say that you simply want to lose weight and you commit to losing a specific number, like 10 pounds in 10 weeks, your chances of hitting that goal skyrocket. This is because you've clearly defined your goal with a number and now you can track your progress towards your goal. This will help you stay focused on exactly what you need to do, which is to lose one pound per week. Then you can track your progress towards that goal and determine how much time you should spend at the gym to achieve it. Weighing yourself everyday will let you track your progress and see if adjustments are needed such as increasing your time at the gym or minimizing the number of calories you consume each day. Now your mindset is much more solid because your goal is clearly defined.

The beauty of this analogy is that it relates so well to financial planning because there are two things in life you can't cheat – your body and your finances. I like to compare financial planning to a bodybuilder. When I meet with a new client for the first time, the first thing I tell them is that I'm a financial fitness coach and my job is to train them to become a financial bodybuilder. To understand where a client is at in their life and determine a plan of action to help them achieve their goals, I work with them to complete a full financial physical. A fitness coach helps you set goals and figure out specifics like what foods your body will need, what sort of exercise you should be doing, and what timeframe you have in mind before you're ready to step on the stage and flex. As a financial fitness coach, when I get a look at an individual's specific financial situation, I can help them determine how to get in their best shape financially.

An important part of a healthy financial mindset involves being honest with who you really are. We're all impulsive, emotional, and at times messy, so developing an overly restrictive budget that won't allow for the occasional impulse can derail your efforts towards financial improvement. Just like a super restrictive diet can lead to stronger impulses to stray from the meal plan, tight financial restrictions can cause you to quit following your budget or give up altogether. This is because feeling deprived can cause you to dislike your own efforts and act impulsively. Knowing your impulsive vices and creating a plan to reduce them in a healthy way while still rewarding yourself occasionally is a crucial part of a positive financial mindset. There's nothing wrong with enjoying a new pair of shoes or taking a night out on the town to reward yourself while you continue working towards financial wellness.

You can find 90% of what you need to do for proper money management online. There are many forums, countless YouTube videos, and many blogs you can Google. They even have smart phone apps that can assist you in creating a basic budget and crunch numbers to tell you how much you need to save for your future. These same tools apply for becoming a bodybuilder, but there's one thing that no amount of apps or YouTube videos can do and that's hold you accountable. The purpose of a coach whether it's with fitness or finances, is to help you learn what investments are best for you and to help you stay focused on your goals. That's why fitness coaches and financial advisors exist – to help you evaluate your current situation, determine your action steps for your specific goals, and ultimately hold you accountable and ensure you follow through on what you've set out to do. That's not to say that an app or video can't be a great starting point, but on the days, you aren't feeling up to going to the gym or reviewing your budget, you need someone to slap the cheat meal right out of your hand. We're all human and we all struggle with being disciplined on a regular basis which is why one of the most important roles of a fitness coach or financial advisor is to talk you through a decision and rationalize the effects of straying from your plan.

The path to achieving your financial goals will never be a straight line which is why it's important to be open to changing your behaviors. Accepting and embracing change will allow you to remain confident on your strategy to achieve your goals and keep a positive mindset. While you can't control certain things like when the market takes a downward turn, you can control your mindset and the strategies you trust to make the best decisions for your future. It's especially important to stay the course and maintain your focus on the positive outcomes of your goals in the beginning of your financial journey. Figure out what steps you need to take to keep yourself motivated for the next 1, 5, 10, or even 20 years. Your target will always be moving but if you keep yourself motivated and keep your ultimate end goal in mind, you can stay on the right path towards that target. Some people use vision boards and goal charts to remind themselves of what they're working towards, but you can do what works best for you and keeps you motivated in a natural and effective way.

Remember that there is no such thing as being done. Life is defined by challenges and learning. A poor mindset believes that one day you'll be able to retire and kick your feet up and do nothing because your hard work is simply paying your dues for a life of leisure. Ironically this is the kind of mindset that stifles the ambition and drive required to ever get to the point of having a future that pays you when you no longer work. When you retire, you will still need to maintain your financial home and manage your investments. Just like with the gym, once you attain your physique, you don't simply stop going to the gym and eating health. Instead, you must continue to maintain your body and your lifestyle. The same holds true with your finances, just ask MC Hammer and Jim Hayes.

As you're working towards your goals, it's important to always be grateful for what you currently have. Too many people focus on feeling resentment towards their status or the circumstances that got them in their current position. Taking action and keeping a positive attitude can help you more than any negative emotions or thoughts. Rather than being resentful of other people that are further along on their financial journey than you are, celebrate their good fortune and focus on improving yourself to contribute to a better world overall. You are your own most valuable asset.

Remember that financial freedom is achieved through your own mindset and your commitment to accountability with your progress and goals. Once you have your financial goals in mind, you should start looking for a financial advisor to help you stay motivated and educated. Many people are self-motivated but most of us need some sort of external motivation especially in our weakest moments. If nothing else, hiring a financial advisor can keep you committed to the financial habits that are the keys to your long-term success.

Exercise 6:
Visualizing Your Goals

I want you to write down a list of your goals, whatever they may be, being as specific as possible.

What do you want to accomplish by the end of next week, next month, and next year?

What do you want to accomplish in 5, 10, and 15 years?

What do you hope to achieve in 20 years?

Now under each goal I want you to write down some steps you can take to achieve each of one. Maybe you want to increase your cash flow, limit your expenses, or start saving more money each paycheck.

Once you have your goals written down and a few steps on how to achieve them, I want you to review them weekly. I want you to ask yourself, what are you doing each week that will get you one step closer to each of your goals? By consistently reviewing your goals and tracking your progress towards each of them, the probability of your success on achieving each goal will skyrocket.

Doing this exercise will give you a better understanding of what you need to do to achieve these goals. This exercise should also help you understand your values and what's important to you. Now you can start to formulate a plan of how you will achieve your goals!

"I believe that the biggest mistake that most people make when it comes to their retirement is they do not plan for it. They take the same route as Alice in the story, Alice in Wonderland, in which the cat tells Alice that surely, she will get somewhere as long as she walks long enough. It may not be exactly where you wanted to get to, but you certainly get somewhere."

Mark Singer

Chapter 12

Your Financial Fitness Coach

I'm willing to bet that before reading this book, you thought you didn't need a financial advisor because you're still in debt, possibly struggling to make ends meet each month, or feel that you can handle it on your own. The reality is that if you were already working with one, you probably would be in a much better financial position by now. Financial advisors can offer a tremendous amount of value by instilling in you the proper mindset, teaching you to formulate and track goals, explaining investment choices, and helping to manage your emotions to make the best financial decisions for your future.

It's important to know that not all financial advisors are created equal and there are a few things you should keep in mind when choosing one. Unfortunately, financial advisors often get a bad rap because many people assume we only cater to the wealthy or that we're only in the finance industry to make a buck for ourselves. Maybe that's true for some financial advisors, but I can tell you there are plenty, like me, that are genuinely working to help as many people as we can. Money management and financial planning are powerful tools that can build a better quality of life and I wish more financial advisors were as passionate as I am when it comes to teaching millennials to use those tools to their benefit.

A few years ago, I noticed the lack of focus in my industry towards millennials for providing guidance in money management, financial planning, and investing. As I began working with my closest friends, I realized how much help our generation needs and that I had the potential to make a huge impact for a lot of millennials. The financial industry is guilty of focusing more intensely on our parents and grandparents, as that is where the money seems to be. While I can understand this business decision, I feel that our generation needs just as much, if not more help and guidance so that we don't throw our future paychecks and potential inheritances down the drain.

As I mentioned, financial planning is very much like personal fitness and bodybuilding. If you want to reach your peak physical form, having a coach that understands your needs and goals along with the knowledge of the industry, is a huge advantage over attempting to do it all yourself. The definition of a financial advisor is someone that helps you create strategies for eliminating financial risk and building wealth over the long term. Simply put, financial advisors help you with all types of financial planning. That means we can help you with everything from budgeting to saving for retirement. At the end of the day, a financial advisor is someone that will hold you accountable and makes sure that you achieve your goals, whatever they may be.

The biggest concern I have for any new client is that they view me the same way they view going to a dentist, with hesitation. Working with a financial advisor does not have to be boring or a chore. This should be a fun process and one that you look forward to participating in. I take priding in letting all my clients know that not only am I here for them as their advisor, but also as a friend. I'm not just a man behind the computer screen or phone that tells you how to invest your money, I'm your personal financial fitness coach, guiding you through anything you need help with and acting as a support system and someone you can talk to.

Right now, only 52% of pre-retirees (ages 50-65) and 44% of retirees (over age 65) consult with a financial advisor[48]. For us millennials, only 11% consult with a financial advisor in any way[49]. A recent study concluded that those who actively worked with a financial advisor and engaged in financial planning, accumulated nearly 250% more retirement savings than those without a financial plan in place. Furthermore, nearly 44% of those who have a financial plan in place save more money each year for retirement[50].

---

[48] 2013 Risks and Process of Retirement Survey Report

[49] 2018 Millennial Saving & Investing Habits survey

[50] 2013 Risks and Process of Retirement Survey Report

Researchers have attempted to quantify into real numbers the value that a proper financial advisor can provide in your life. Their research shows that financial advisors help individuals generate roughly 1.82% excess return each year, creating roughly 29% higher retirement income. The proof is there that working with a financial advisor can make a positive impact on your life.

To find a financial advisor that fits you and your needs, begin by searching for someone that is close in age and able to relate to your current lifestyle, values, and vision of wealth. I recommend that you find a financial advisor whose age is within 10 years of your own, as this allows them to better understand your general life circumstances, so they can connect with you not only on a professional level but also a personal level. We're all busy these days, and for most millennials, working long hours, raising families, or travelling can make scheduling appointments difficult. Finding a financial advisor that can work with your schedule and employs technology like virtual meetings, can allow you to interact with us even if you're on the other side of the country. The most important thing to look for in a financial advisor is someone who can fit your lifestyle and your availability.

Look for an advisor that is going to view all your goals with a holistic approach and think about the big picture. Look for the financial advisor who will help you design and build your financial home by helping you to pour the foundation, construct the first floor, build steps to the second floor, and lay shingles on the roof. More than half of financial planning may have nothing to do with investing, but instead focus on planning an affordable vacation for your family, preparing to pay your child's college tuition, or even choosing the best vehicle to purchase. A financial advisor can even work with you to determine the best credit card to get or provide you with career and business advice.

So, when you're searching for a financial advisor, look for one who specializes in working with millennials and someone who listens and can respond to you and your own goals because after all, everyone is different and has a different path. Spending a few hours each year with someone to hold you accountable, review your goals, and help adjust your plan, can allow you to stay on track and attain your lifestyle and the freedom you desire.

Most millennials could benefit greatly from talking with a financial advisor as they try to figure out the best way to make money, save money, and live life on their own terms. For me, being a financial advisor is about doing what it takes to help make YOU more successful and this includes not only helping you with decisions, but also pointing you in the right direction. Financial planning is about a lot more than just money because you have your own unique goals and at the end of the day, money is simply a tool to help you accomplish them. I hope that by reading this chapter, you have a better understanding of the purpose of a financial advisor and how finding the right one can greatly benefit you both now and in the future.

"Dream big, work hard, never give up"

Jonathan Turner, Hopeful Best-Selling Author

Final Thoughts

Navigating your finances in the world we live in today can be overwhelming to even think about let alone actually take action to fix. If our conversation has given you a better understanding about the challenges we face, allowed you to define what wealth means to you, helped you to better manage your finances, and given you a basic understanding of investing, then I've succeeded with the purpose of this book. Your path to financial freedom may look different than someone else's, but if you're moving forward on that path, you have a better chance of succeeding than if you choose to avoid it and continue struggling financially.

What I truly want you to take away from my book is the feeling of hope for your future, confidence in your abilities to make changes, and motivation to take action immediately so you can achieve financial freedom, however you choose to define it. Remember how important it is to keep the proper mindset and structure to your life and be sure to define your vision of retirement, whether it's spending time with your family, travelling, or driving around in your dream car. Always keep in mind that some lifestyles are more expensive to support than others, so you should choose your future lifestyle wisely.

Money provides a means to an end, nothing more, but proper money management and financial planning give you the ability to harness money for its true potential. Despite what you may have learned, this won't be an easy road and you won't see a dramatic change overnight. Embrace the delayed gratification, knowing that over the coming decades, you'll be able to do what you want, when you want. Take what you've learned as a compass towards a brighter future and allow our conversation to guide you in the right direction. Let a solid financial plan be the map to navigate your path and attain your goals. Don't be afraid to seek advice especially from a financial advisor who can hold you accountable on your journey. Chances are we have not yet had the pleasure of meeting in person, but I would love to hear from you. After these closing thoughts, I have dedicated a page to finding me on social media so give me a follow and feel free to message me! Now cue the upbeat, motivational music as I leave you with my parting thoughts.

As I've said before, to me, money represents nothing more and nothing less than freedom. Money allows us the freedom to pursue the life we desire, the freedom to do what we want, when we want, and the security of earning a paycheck when we no longer want to work for one.

"It takes 20 years to build a reputation and five minutes to ruin it. If you think about that, you'll do things differently."
– Warren Buffet

Have you ever thought about the legacy you want to leave behind? How you make people feel along the way as you journey to your destination is just as important as the journey itself. This is something my father taught me many years ago, instilling in me to assume someone is watching everything I do. I bring that lesson with me where ever I go and now I share it with you. Leave a great legacy behind – be true to your word, don't partake in gossip, and never cheat to get ahead. Find your inspiration and motivation from those you admire most and strive to make them proud. For me, there is no greater gift that I could give my parents than to grow the business they started many years ago into something they have only ever dreamed of.

At long last I'll leave you with my final words of wisdom…

"I am Iron Man!"

Shit, wrong story. Let me try that again…

"Start planning your future, today!"

STOP FAKING IT, START MAKING IT

Where You Can Find Me

I'd love to hear from you! It would be an honor if you could share this book with your friends and leave me an online review from wherever you purchased it. I hope this book creates a positive impact in your life and helps you to attain your vision of wealth. We only get one shot in this life, make it worth it!

Sincerely,
Jonathan Turner

Where you can find me online:

www.startmakingit.com
Instagram.com/jonathan_m_turner
Youtube.com/c/JonathanTurnerVideos

Acknowledgements

Writing a book is harder than I thought and more rewarding than I could have ever imagined. None of this would have been possible without the continued love, support, and encouragement from my wife, Olivia. From reading every single draft of the book, cooking me dinners while I spent countless nights in front of my computer typing away, to motivating me to continue in the times that I felt lost, she has helped me realize my potential in writing this book and I cannot thank her enough. Love you babe!

I'm forever grateful to my parents, Charles and Deborah Turner. From an early age, you have each led by example what it means to dedicate yourself to something that your passionate about and let nothing stand in your way. For all of the year's that I caused a few pieces of hair to fall out or possibly turn gray ahead of schedule, I hope that I have shown the both of you that you each succeeded in raising me to become the man I am today. One day when Olivia and I have children, if we are even half as successful as the both of you were with Michael and myself, I'd feel accomplished.

To Dave and Angela Madeira, allowing me to marry your daughter Olivia has been the single greatest thing to happen to me. I want to thank the both of you for accepting me into your family and for all of your help in the process of writing this book, from your continued support to the countless drafts I forced you to read.

What happens when you have trouble making your book flow in a cohesive order? You call Ellen Ross. I cannot thank Ellen enough for all of her help in the endeavor. Ellen has been a crucial part in me keeping my sanity throughout this process, possibly at the expense of her own. We spent many weeks emailing, texting, and speaking on the phone numerous times a day making this book what it is today. Ellen, you truly have no idea how much I appreciate all of your help on this book!

STOP FAKING IT, START MAKING IT

What is a great book without a great cover design and informative graphics? I want to thank Anthony Cataldi and his company at Studio27 Print & Design for the kickass cover design and the amazing work on all of the graphics in this book. Anthony and I spent numerous hours sitting on web meetings while he designed the cover and the graphics to get everything just right. I truly appreciate all of his work in designing the best cover and informative graphics that I could imagined!

Finally, to all of my family and friends that supported my idea of writing a book and reached out with continued encouragement during the process, thank you!